fragments

MARILYN MONROE
fragments
poems, intimate notes, letters

EDITED BY
STANLEY BUCHTHAL
AND
BERNARD COMMENT

harpercollins publishers ltd

Photograph credits can be found on page 239.

HarperCollins books may be purchased for educational, business, or sales promotional use through our Special Markets Department.

HarperCollins Publishers Ltd
2 Bloor Street East, 20th Floor
Toronto, Ontario, Canada
M4W 1A8

www.harpercollins.ca

Library and Archives Canada Cataloguing in Publication information is available upon request

ISBN: 978-1-44340-268-2

Designed by Valérie Gautier

Printed in the United States of America
10   9   8   7   6   5   4   3   2   1

CONTENTS

EDITORS' NOTE

Norma Jeane Mortenson was born under the sign of Gemini, and she described herself as having two natures: "Jekyll and Hyde, two in one." Even the initials of her stage name (which, according to one story, were suggested to her by the clearly visible "M"s formed by the lines of her palms) supported this duality, as did the pseudonym, Zelda Zonk, that she used while escaping incognito from Hollywood to New York.

In her lifetime, under pressure from the studios, the media created a joyful and radiant image of Marilyn Monroe, even to the point of making her out to be a "dumb blonde." One remembers her parts in *Gentlemen Prefer Blondes*, *The Seven Year Itch*, *How to Marry a Millionaire*, and *Let's Make Love*. Anything contrary to this artificial image was not welcome. There was no room for a melancholic Marilyn. The icon was not allowed to have an opposite side.

Yet, like a medal, she did have two sides. The sunny and luminous one of the sparkling blonde, and the darker one of the excessive perfectionist who sought absolutes and for whom life (work, friendships, and love affairs) could only lead to disappointment. "I think I have a gay side in me and also a sad side," Marilyn confided in an interview.

Her friend Marlon Brando expressed perfectly the shock people felt when her death was announced: "Everybody stopped work, and you could see all that day the same expressions on their faces, the same thought: 'How can a girl with success, fame, youth, money, beauty . . . how could she kill herself?' Nobody could understand it because those are the things that everybody wants, and they can't believe that life wasn't important to Marilyn Monroe, or that her life was elsewhere."

Marilyn's hand, 1946

There are thousands of photographs of this icon. Her image has been used in many, sometimes brutal, ways. But in this book a new world of truthfulness and overwhelming clarity is being thrown open. A hitherto unknown and unseen Marilyn is revealed.

On her death in 1962, Marilyn Monroe's personal possessions were bequeathed to Lee Strasberg, and when he in turn died in 1982, his young widow, Anna Strasberg, inherited this large and uncataloged collection, which included dresses, cosmetics, pictures, books, receipts, and so forth. Many years later, while sorting out Lee Strasberg's papers, she found two boxes of poems and other manuscripts written by Marilyn. Not knowing what to do with these, she asked a family friend, Stanley Buchthal, for advice. Some months later, at an art collectors' dinner, Stanley told Bernard Comment, a French essayist and editor, about Anna Strasberg's find in order to get his opinion of the unpublished materials. That was the start of the adventure that became this book.

As far as has been possible to determine, the texts are placed in chronological order. Words printed in red are the editors' and correct spelling mistakes, add missing words, or suggest possible readings of indecipherable words. The ordering of fragments of very disparate documents has been an attempt at reconstruction and hence at interpretation. The flow of Marilyn's thoughts on individual pages, and from one successive page to another, is indicated by red arrows (black arrows are Marilyn's own).

It is possible that other texts written by Marilyn will surface in the years or decades to come. For the moment, this book contains every available text, excepting her technical notes on acting. In any case, these writings reveal a young woman who was dissatisfied with issues of surface appearance and who was seeking the truth at the heart of both things and people.

Only lovers of clichés will be surprised that the Hollywood actress was passionately fond of literature, although this fact cannot be illustrated merely by the pictures collected in this book. (Still: how many actresses from that period do we know who sometimes took pains to be photographed reading or holding a book?) In a 1960 interview with the French journalist Georges Belmont, Marilyn recalled the beginning of her career: "Nobody could imagine what I did when I wasn't shooting, because they didn't see me at previews or premieres or parties. It's simple: I was going to school! I'd never finished high school, so I started going to UCLA at night, because during the day I had small parts in pictures. I took courses in the history of literature and the history of this country, and I started to read a lot, stories by wonderful writers." Her library contained four hundred books, ranging from such classics as Milton, Dostoyevsky, and Whitman to contemporary writers, including Hemingway, Beckett, and Kerouac.

Arthur Miller played a part in her development as a reader, too, recommending Carl Sandburg's six-volume biography of Abraham Lincoln, which she devoured. But some years before they were involved, Marilyn had already tackled James Joyce's *Ulysses*.

As we know, Marilyn inspired numerous painters: Dalí, De Kooning, and Warhol, among others. She also felt a real interest in painting—in the painters of the Italian Renaissance, such as Botticelli; Goya, especially his demons ("I know this man very well, we have the same dreams, I have had the same dreams since I was a child"); Degas, whose ballet dancer she gazed at in wonder when taken to see a private collection; and also Rodin, whose *Hand of God* she admired at length in the Metropolitan Museum of Art.

From all these examples emerges a cultured and curious Marilyn who had a strong desire to understand others, the outside world, destiny, and, of course, herself. She took notes, swiftly setting down her feelings and thoughts and expressing her wonder. Some may be surprised at her spelling mistakes, in which, most probably, a form of dyslexia is detectable. But readers of Marcel Proust's correspondence (Marilyn read *Swann's Way* on the set of *Love Nest* in 1951) will have seen worse. The very Proust who, answering the question "to which failings are you most lenient?" replied unhesitatingly, "spelling mistakes," and who, in one of his letters, wrote this strange and beautiful phrase: "Each spelling mistake is the expression of a desire."

The collection of documents revealed here is nothing less than a treasure trove. We owe its appearance to Anna Strasberg and her sons, Adam and David, who, during the preparation of this book, have embraced the opportunity to uncover a hitherto undervalued, even unknown dimension of Marilyn's personality. From beginning to end we have shared their desire to create a book that, we would like to think, would have pleased its author. Marilyn once confessed to a journalist: "I think Lee probably changed my life more than any other human being. That's why I love to go to the Actors Studio whenever I'm in New York." Perhaps Strasberg, more than other people, had sensed who Marilyn really was.

One of the remarkable insights these documents offer is the sense that

Marilyn was, until the end, planning for the future. Among other projects, she hoped over time to play the great Shakespearean roles, from Juliet to Lady Macbeth. She also pursued her idea of creating a new production company in association with Marlon Brando.

Some texts will give rise to interpretation and comment. But there is nothing dirty or low, no gossip in this book; that was not Marilyn's way. What the notes reveal is intimacy without showiness, the seismic measuring of a soul. They take nothing away from Marilyn's mystery but rather make the mystery more material. She was an elusive star with a magnetic force that sent compasses haywire whenever she got close.

To this day, her face, her eyes, her lips appear all around the world. Innumerable actors and pop singers take her as a reference, a definitive model: to sound like her, to act like her, in advertisements and music videos and films. Songs are composed for her—among them this famous one, by Elton John and Bernie Taupin: "Goodbye Norma Jeane (. . .) / Loneliness was tough / The toughest role you ever played / Hollywood created a superstar / And pain was the price you paid / Even when you died / Oh the press still hounded you / All the papers had to say / Was that Marilyn was found in the nude."

This book does not attempt to show her stripped bare but, rather, simply as she was. Through these poems and written papers, she's more alive than ever.

Stanley Buchthal
Bernard Comment

fragments

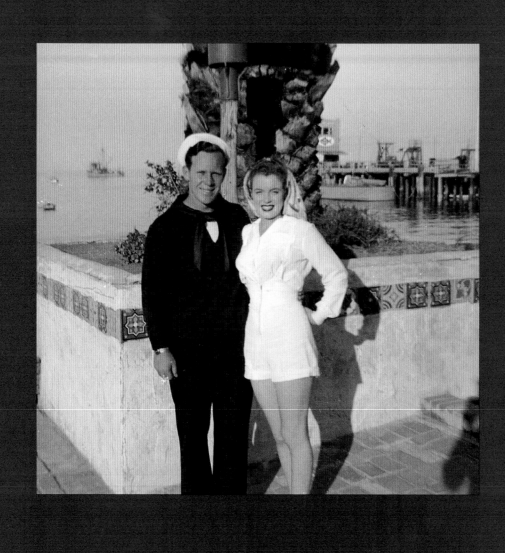

Jim Dougherty and Norma Jeane, Catalina Island, fall of 1943

PERSONAL NOTE
1943

Norma Jeane married James Dougherty when she turned sixteen, the age of consent in California, on June 19, 1942, thereby escaping the threat of being returned to an orphanage when her foster family moved out of state. Dougherty was born in April 1921 and was five years older than she was. At the end of 1943, the young couple settled for a few months on Catalina Island off the coast of Los Angeles, a fashionable resort before the war. It is likely that this long note, uncharacteristically typed, was written at this time.

One can't help being surprised, even impressed, by the maturity of this seventeen-year-old girl, whose feelings of disillusionment are plain from the first sentence, as she examines her marriage and what she expects from life, and faces the fear of her husband's betrayal. Nevertheless, the disjointedness of the text reveals turbulent emotions.

The "other woman" she mentions might be a reference to Doris Ingram, her young husband's former girlfriend and a Santa Barbara beauty queen. The couple were divorced on September 13, 1946.

my relationship with him was basically insecure from the
first night I spent alone with him. He was very insecure
not perhaps so much of himself but of how I a girl 6 yr
younger would react - actually in the beginning I would
never have stayed with him but for his love of classical
music his intellect which made a pretense at being more
then it was and his desire to bring out any maturer
qualities envolving personality or secual relations with
me. It was a period in which I ran up against many doubts
as to whether this young man of 21 was in unreality my
surpressed edea of a dream man - probaleling I was greatly
attracted to him as one of the ~~only~~ few young men I had no
sexual repulsion for besides which it gave me a false sense
of security to feel that he# was endowed with more over-
welming qualities which I did not possess ------ on paper
it all begins to sound terribly logical but the secret mid-
night meetings the fugetive glance stolen in others company
the sharing of the ocean, moon & stars and air aloneness
made it a ~~te~~ romantic adventure ~~for~~ which a young, rather
shy girl who didnt always give that impression because of
her desire to belong & develope can thrive on -- I had always felt a need to live up to that expectation of my elders
having been not ~~a per~~ in a precosious manner an unusually
mature child for my age - and at ~~twel~~ 10, 11, 12 & 13 when
my closer companions were all persons of 4 to 6 yrs - ad-
vancement this envirement of peo. into which I at first
inadvertantly fell made all the problems of adolesance,
that painful inbetween age, where one yearns only to be
accepted in _ones_ _own_ age group, more intensified, so that
at 15, I felt strongly the pattern of insecurity I had
developed -- only ~~we~~ with people younger or older was I
confortable and in such presences I became an advanced
child who fitted in easily except on grounds where her own

- continued -

age group of 15-21) was involved probably my frustrations
are no greater then those of any teenage girl but some overcome it by loosing principle & intelligence to a degree where
I felt that eventually this would combat not conquer for
them. All my unfounded jealousies were surpressed by my
desire to find myself a full person ready to face less
superficial problems then the typical teenager is supposed to
have.

I was a very small delicatly built girl - at 15 I
had done a play T.V. - show a leading part modeling
occasionally with innumerable opportunities movies to
contracts - steady modeling so that to an outsider it might
not be concievable that I had taken my small insecurities
and built them up into a nervous tension which although it
had outlets was always present ~~whi~~ with so some people no
apparent reason. ~~during most of my~~ during the ~~summer ther~~
year there would be days or weeks when I wanted only to have
occasional company when desired - to busy myself in reading
so that any attempt at ajustment to a situation which looked
slightly forboding became an exausting process -- I was an
intense introvert probably but because I loved people and
had friends wherevere I cared to cultivate them it was perhaps balanced more then it might be. -- if I had not any
agreeable or charming social patterns the unfortunate
thing was that any/ or coldness withdrawing was deliberate and that although I recognized this feeling I had no desire except in
very passionate moods to overcome my feelings -- very few
people except my more sensitive acuaintences sensed this
and accepted it fully he did not - for being in himself a
person who had in different envirement my problems to a
lesser degree.

- 2 -

One experiance which I have not analized
objectively nor will I probably be able to occured one evening - the past night we had spent together my being in a
bitchy withdrawn mood the evening was rather weary and
weighted with almost a distrust of him & his relation to
this other girl which I at first would only aproach (and not
to accept in a very roundabout manner so that we parted
rather cooly and abruptly making no plans to meet ~~seeretly~~
the next night, I being the romantic estheticl soul I am
believed that like some great lover he would know I was waiting for him unfortunaly he did not appear and I began to be-
rate him & myself - myself for being unrealistic ~~n~~ mean
undomonstretive and for allowing myself to care in a situation I felt I had been drawn into and then forced to grow
with first by he then by my consious being slowly falling
into the habits which my actions set -

I think that only a person who remembers growing
up might very clearly & completely see what an objective
analitical view I an trying to establish suceeding in becoming a trifle to pompass about my own reletively simple
thoughts but then its very difficult for me to set down on
paper as if talking to a second person those bare truths &
emotions I felt - perhaps even poetic but which if I wrote
them in thier naturl form I fear I might disgard right into
the wastepaper basket -

note) listening to the little girl crying in the
hall it seems that at times children have remarkable per-
seption & ~~insite~~ insight and in some even a very humane
trait which while in the prosess of growing up one loses
touch with - (oh damn! I get so carried away that I
completely sidetrack myself good intentions or no) anyway
finding myself ofhandedly stood up snubbed my first feeling
was not of anger - but the numb pain of rejection & hurt at

the (destruction ~~of~~ of some sort of edealistic image of
true love.

My first impulse then was one of complete sub-
jection humiliation, alonement to the male counterpart.
(all this thought & writting has made my hands tremble but
I just want to keep pouring it out until that great pot in
the mind is, though not emptied, ~~relieves~~ relieved - I know
when I sit down & read this I will blanche at the thought
of having written so much crap - (you see side-tracked
again) - then - out of sheer desparation I sopose I stood &
waiting for one hour & a quarter suffering as greatly &
though not as ~~notel~~ notebly or sobbing as Duses & crying
not hystericaly ~~but~~ just large drops ~~fal~~ trickling down my
nose making me scratch my face - underneath I was worried
that he might come & see me in that piteful state eyes red-
nose shinning hair falling stragling curtaining one eye
<u>end of</u>
evening.

Then came the 2nd act while speaking - rather she
spoke (one of those I had been avoiding I discovered & that
he had spent the evening & most of the morning hours with
the <u>other woman</u> to be prosaic & I thanked God I had waylaid
him on the beach to protest my und^{ie}ying love - rejection I
could endure but making a fool of myself even if he had
been sincere in his love ~~I could~~ my pride could not take -
also the fact that I was so foolishly loyal and that I did
not have a chance to wound him in some childish fashion
was another blow to my as yet unsteady ego - I now would
like a chance at a third act - the unsuspecting male and
~~then~~ the vengful female, ~~et~~ but now I'm only fooling myself if I do get my last act I will portray the heroine
who bravely suffers tucking it all away to use as barage
~~form~~ some now unknown man.

- 4 -

(this is all making me feel easier and perhaps
spending the night alone will not be a trial such as the
one I forced myself through last night - I would like to
see him though as I'm leaving this place tomorrow - why
isn't anything plain & commonplace ordinary & easy -

I guess I'm to emotional in the wrong spots -

but if things weren't like that I would probably
bore myself - although if I were different I would hardly
know the defference (I've been smoking and it is a filthy
habit (it's not one of mine yet) I have the most unpleasant
smell and ~~tel~~ taste in my mouth as if I ~~were~~ had chewed raw
tobacco over a sustained amount of time.

Why is it that after all this sensible talk the
thought of meeting him still not uncovering my feelings
makes my pulse beat and I feel the blood flush my body (if
I had any sense disipline or courage I would not even look
for the boy who won't be there yet I know know that at 12
o clock I will feel another surge of resentment).

I think my love if you must call it that was
mostly that wonderful titulaling feeling of of being wanted,
loved & cared for ~~by-a~~ & any sexual ~~attach~~ attraction.

~~I-thing~~ I think perhaps I would be freer tonight
& might even be able to say I love you looking into his eyes
straight & feeling a tinge of hate or something akin to it.

to show its my feminine being that wants satisfaction last night I was so badly sunburnt that I wore only
a sweater & no bra - it gave me a sensual feeling I thought
he ~~my~~ might share - now there is the question of whether he
lied to me - if he loved us both I could accept that but
if he lied when he said I was first & foremost and that if
this relationship ever differed he would share this information with me for as he himself said, I would not want to
play second fiddle.

- 5 -

There is one span of time in which I knew he was
honest but then she had not ~~met~~ entered _our_ lives - (as you
see I am still quite an optomist and soon I hope I can
laugh about this - ~~e~~ laughter without that protective false
ring.

Its hard not to try and rationalize and protect
your own feelings but eventually that makes the acceptance
of truth more difficult -

And I was planning to come here for two weeks -
if I do the play I can go through 2 weeks of hell but if
not I either have to make a very fast adjustment or find
another vacation spot.

For someone like me its wrong to go through ~~threw~~
thorough self analisis - I do it enough in thought
generalities enough.

Its not to much fun to know yourself to well or
think you do - everyone needs a little conciet to carry
them ~~past the~~ through & past the falls

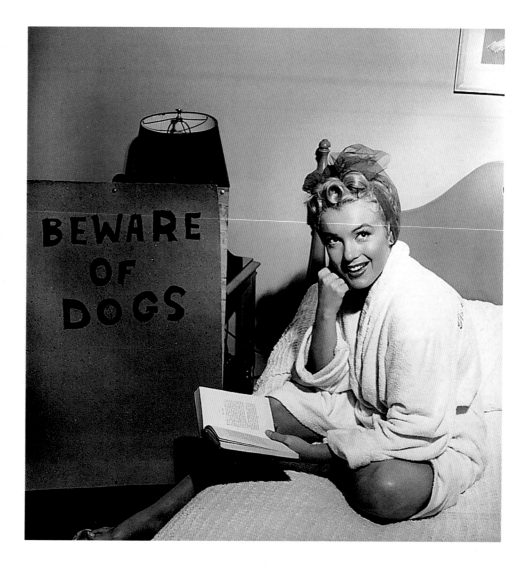

Marilyn during the filming of *Niagara*, 1952
Marilyn reading Heinrich Heine

Marilyn in the garden of Hotel Bel-Air, Los Angeles, 1952
Marilyn reading Joyce's *Ulysses*, Long Island, summer of 1955

stretch
expansion
(open) (free)

Keep the
rule
   To begin
    with
     a ray
   tension

Keep the balloon
And
Dare not to worry
Dare to
let go—so loose
Then you pick up
Stretch into your tone

Sense of humor
Keeping a giggle inside

Let go of my
eyes—
so relaxed
only let
my thought
come through
them without
doing any
thing to
them

stretch
expantion
open tree

hit the cue

to begin with a new tempo

Beverly Hills Hotel

Keep the balloon

And

Dare not to worry

Dare to
let go - so loose
Then you pick up
stretch into your tone

sense of humor
Keeping a giggle inside

let go of
my eyes -
so relaxed
only let
my though
some through
Them without
doing any
thing to
them

On Hospital gowns

My bare
(darrie) derrière
is out ~~the air~~
in the air
when I'm not aware
aware
several
Handel Concertos
Vivaldi Concertos
Benny Goodman

My (pair)

Beethoven
Last 6—quartets
Ravel—the Waltz
Bartok—quartets of his
continued on other side
of list of records

on Hospital gowns
my bare
clarie derrière
is out
in the Air
which I'm not aware
aware
several
Handel Concertos

Vivaldi Concertos

Benny Goodman

My

Last 6 — Beetovean
Quartets
Reval — the wath
Bartok — quartets of his
Continued on other side
of list of records

I can't really stand Human
Beings sometimes—I know
they all have their problems
as I have mine—but I'm really
too tired for it. Trying to understand,
making allowances, seeing certain things
that just weary me.

I can't really stand Human
Beings sometimes - I Know
they all have their problems
as I have mine - but I'm really
too tired for it. Trying to understand,
making allowances, seeing certain things
that just weary me.

Only parts of us will ever
touch ~~only~~ parts of others—
one's own truth is just
that really—<u>one's</u> own truth.
We can only share the
part that <u>is</u> ~~understood by~~ within another's knowing acceptable ~~to
the other   therefore~~ so one
is for most part <u>alone</u>.
As it is meant to be in
evidently in nature—at best ~~though~~ perhaps it could make
our understanding seek
another's loneliness out.

Only parts of us will ever touch only parts of others — ones own truth is just that really — ones own truth.

We can only share the part that is within anothers understanding knowing acceptable to the other — therefore so one is for most part alone.

As it is meant to be in prudently in nature — at best perhaps it would make our understanding seek anothers loneliness out.

Stones on the walk
every color there is
I stare down at you
like ~~those the~~ a horizon—
the space / the air is between us beckoning
and I am many stories ~~besides~~ up
my feet ~~are~~ frightened
~~from my~~ as I grasp ~~for~~ towards you

stones on the walk
every color there is
I stare down at you
like there a hirizon —
                                    beckoning
the space is between us beckoning
and I am
and many stories up writes —
my feet   frieghtened
  as
from my grasp to swinds you

Oh damn I wish that I were
dead—absolutely nonexistent—
gone away from here—from
everywhere but how would I ~~do it~~
There is always bridges—the Brooklyn
bridge ~~no not the Brooklyn Bridge~~
~~because~~ But I love that bridge (everything is beautiful from there
                        and the air is so clean) walking it seems
peaceful ~~there~~ even with all those
cars going crazy underneath. So
it would have to be some other bridge
an ugly one and with no view—except
I ~~particularly~~ like in particular all bridges—there's something about them and besides ~~these~~ I've
never seen an ugly bridge

Oh damn, I wish that I were dead - Absolutly non existant, gone away from here - from everywhere's how would I ~~death~~ There is always bridges - the Brooklyn Bridge - ~~He not the Brooklyn bridge~~ ~~because~~ But I love that bridge every unthinkable thing from that & the air is so clean it seems peaceful ~~there~~ even with all those cars going crazy under neathe - So it would have to be some other bridge an ugly one "n" with no view - except I ~~really~~ like in particular all bridges - theres something about them and besides ~~there I've~~ never seen an ugly bridge

Life—
I am of both of your directions
~~Life~~
Somehow remaining hanging downward
the most
but strong as a cobweb in the
wind—I exist more with the cold glistening frost.
But my beaded rays have the colors I've
seen in a paintings—ah life they
have cheated you

Note: Marilyn apparently wrote several variations on the theme of the twofold course of life ("life in both directions") and the delicate, sometimes invisible "cobweb," revealed by dew and resistant to wind—in particular a poem entitled "To the Weeping Willow" that was published in Norman Rosten's book about Marilyn: "I stood beneath your limbs / And you flowered and finally / clung to me, / and when the wind struck with the earth / and sand—you clung to me. / Thinner than a cobweb I, / sheerer than any— / but it did attach itself / and held fast in strong winds / life—of which at singular times / I am both of your directions— / somehow I remain hanging downward the most, / as both of your directions pull me."

Life, ——

1 am of both of your directions

~~Life~~

Somehow remaining *hanging* downward
the most

but strong as a cobweb in the
wind – 1 exist *more* with the ~~od~~ glistening frost.
~~but~~ my beaded rays have *the* colors I've
seen in a painting – ah life they
have cheated you

UNDATED POEMS

Marilyn Monroe wrote poemlike texts or fragments on loose-leaf paper and in notebooks. She showed her work only to intimate friends, in particular to Norman Rosten, a college friend of Arthur Miller with whom she became very close. A Brooklyn-based novelist, he encouraged Marilyn to continue writing. In the book he wrote about her (*Marilyn Among Friends*), he concluded, "She had the instinct and reflexes of the poet, but she lacked the control."

It is likely that the poetic form, or more generally the fragment, allowed her to express short, lightning bursts of feeling—but who could hear that frail voice, the very opposite of the radiant star? Arthur Miller wrote strikingly: "To have survived, she would have had to be either more cynical or even further from reality than she was. Instead, she was a poet on a street corner trying to recite to a crowd pulling at her clothes."

"RECORD" BLACK NOTEBOOK

AROUND 1951

As she often did, Marilyn filled only a few pages of this notebook, about twelve out of the hundred and fifty it contains and at obviously distinct periods. The first pages open with a heartfelt "Alone!!!" followed by reflections on fear and feelings that can't be put into words; these were probably jotted down in response to acting classes, which may have been those given by Michael Chekhov that she started attending in September 1951. On page 135 of the notebook, there is a poignant text about the panicky fear that sometimes overtook her when she was about to shoot a scene because of her dread of disappointing; her deep-seated sense that, despite the good work she had done, the bad outweighed it, sapping her confidence. Here the language is very strong: "depressed mad."

On page 146, she jotted down in pencil one of the few lines she delivered in *Love Nest* (1951), a film by Joseph M. Newman, in the supporting but nonetheless crucial role of Roberta Stevens, who was the former wartime (girl?)friend of the hero, Jim Scott.

The notes on pages 148 and 149 of the notebook indicate diligent reading on the Florentine Renaissance, unless they are class notes from courses she attended at UCLA in the fall of 1950, after she had already begun acting in films. However, this school-like exercise is surrounded by an older story that most likely preceded her star status, as she writes of traveling in a crowded bus. Could this have been the same bus in which she met sixty likable Italian sailors, then a headily perfumed Filipino boy, ending up, half-crushed by a sleeping five-year-old almost slipping from his young mother's arms, in the middle of sailors far too young to feel sad?

Alone !!?!!

I am alone I am always
                    Alone
no matter what

Look May
Hu 2729
Rupert Allen

There is nothing to fear
but fear itself

What do I believe in +
              What is truth?
I believe in my self
even my most delicate
intangible feeling
in the end Everything is
intangible
                  most
my precious liquid must
never spill   don't spill your
                   precious liquid
              life force
They are all my feelings
No matter what

My feeling doesn't
happen to swell
into words -

Alone!!!!!
I am alone—I am always
alone
no matter what.

Look Mag
Hu 27291
Rupert Allan

There is nothing to fear
but fear itself

What do I believe in
What is truth
I believe in myself
even my most delicate
intangible feelings
in the end everything is
intangible
my most precious liquid must
never spill don't spill your precious liquid
life force
they are all my feelings
no matter what

My feeling doesn't
happen to swell
into words—

Note: Rupert Allan met Marilyn in 1959. As the
West Coast editor of *Look* magazine, he had
secured Marilyn her first cover photo, which
appeared on June 3, 1952. This may explain
her reference "Look Mag." Subsequently,
Rupert Allan became Marilyn's press agent and
remained such up until the end of the filming of
The Misfits, when he accepted Grace Kelly's offer
to work for her in Monaco.

actress must have no feel — no feel — mouth

focus my thought on the picture

feeling in the end of my fingers

Nothing must come — between me and my part — my feeling — concentration

The feeling only getting rid of everything else

letting go — no looks — face only — feeling

3

No Attitude

listening to the lady for the feeling.

listen with the eyes

buoyancy

Tension

love — having no brakes
letting go of everything
feeling only — all I have to do is think it. How do

I hear the melody — the

Tone springs from emotion

Tone — groans and moans "I'm
(animals — down to the frogs")

so sick" — hums from

With Cat — hum — nice kitty
starts from below my feet
feet — all in my feet

Actress must have no mouth
no feet
shoulder
girdle hangs light
hanging
so-o-o
loose
everything
focus my thought on
the partner—
feeling in the end of
my fingers

~~Nothing must come~~
~~between me and my~~
~~part—my feeling—~~
~~concentration~~
The feeling only
getting rid of everything
else
my mind speaks
no looks
body only
letting go—face feeling
mind
spirit

<u>no</u> attitude
listening to the body for
the feeling
listen with the eyes
buoyancy
Tension
loose—having <u>no brakes</u>
letting go of everything.
feeling only—<u>all I have to</u>
<u>do is think it.</u> How do
I hear the melody—the
Tone springs from emotion
Tone—groans and moans—"I'm
          (animals—"down to the hogs")
so sick"—hums from
with cat—hum—nice kitty soft.

starts from below my feet
feet—all in my feet.

What is my pantomime playing with
How is my head?

as if I might never
speak   more

transparency
letting go
down down in back
pulling up from here
right tension

as if I might never
speak   move

transparency.
letting go.
down down in back.
pulling up from here.
right tension   stomach
[illegible] only

Fear of giving me the lines anew
maybe won't be able to learn them
maybe will make mistake
people will either think I'm
no good or laugh or
belittle me or think I
can't act
Women looked stern and
critical - unfriendly and
cold in general
afraid director won't think I'm
very good -
Remembering when I
couldn't do a God damn
thing
Keep trying to build
myself up with the
fact that I have done
things right that were
even good and have
had moments that
were excellent but
the load is heavier
to carry around and
feel less no confidence
depressed (me)

Fear of giving me the lines new
maybe won't be able to learn them
maybe I'll make mistakes
people will either think I'm no good or
laugh or belittle me or think I can't act.
Women looked stern and critical—
unfriendly and cold in general
afraid director won't think I'm any good.
remembering when I couldn't do a god
damn thing.
then trying to build myself up with the
fact that I have done things right that
were even good and have had moments
that were excellent but the bad is heavier
to carry around and feel have no confidence
depressed mad

146

Pardon me
are you the janitors
wife

147

caught the Greyhound
there Bus from Monterey
to Salinas on the
Bus I was the only person
woman with about
fifty italian fisherman
and he never met
sixty such charming gentleman — they
were wonderful some
company was sending them
down state where their boats
and fish (they hoped) were
waiting for them. Some
could hardly speak english
not only do I love Greeks
I love Italians —
their warm, lusty and friendly
as hell — I'd love to go to
Italy some day.

Pardon me
are you the janitor's
wife

caught a Greyhound
Bus from Monterey
to Salinas. On the
Bus I was the ~~only~~ person
woman with about
sixty italian fishermen
and I've never met
sixty such charming gentlemen—they
were wonderful. Some
company was sending them
downstate where their boats
and (they hoped) fish were
waiting for them. Some
could hardly speak english
not only do I love Greeks
[illegible] I love Italians.
they're ~~so~~ warm, lusty and friendly
as hell—I'd love to go to
Italy someday.

Notes:
The sentence on page 146 of the notebook is one
of the few lines Marilyn had to say in *Love Nest*
(1951), so we may assume that these notes—at
any rate, the ones written in pencil—date from the
same period.

In February 1948, Marilyn went to the California
towns of Salinas and Castroville in order to
promote diamond sales in two jewelry stores.
She stayed at the Jeffery Hotel in Salinas for a
week.

Medici 1400 AD-1748
prototype - first type
first foundling home

Giovanni di Bici
Bronze doors in the
in Florence
used his~~ ~~ Ghiberti 23 1424 perspective
great Achilles Brunelleschi 22
Donatello 1386 - 1466
Masaccio 1401-1428
   father of modern art (realistic
poverty Careless about his painting)
life except his painting
Giovanni di Bici responsible
for him. his work never recognized
until after his death.
The Pantheon - Temple
Greek philosophy - golden mean
matters too big a treasure
kept out the old pope
gave money for temples for Brunelleschi
elected him Signoria
Gonfaloniere (governing body)
(grd)

Giovanni di Bici
                    d 1428

Cosimo - Pater Patriae   Lorenzo
1424 - first Public Library

Piero   Giovanni
Lorenzo the Magnificent   Giuliano

Machiavelli
1469 - 1527
Botticelli

damn near broke my back
and disappointed my back too not to sleep
trying to sleep
too ✓

poured my seat when a
cat left the lazy the
only empty seat so
I left more for the
girl could sit her but
down and I took the
other seat. It was next
to a philippino boy and
he smelled good like
~~flowers~~ flowers

Medici 1400 AD–1748
Prototype—first type
Giovanni di Bicci first foundling home
Bronze doors in the
in Florence 1424
Ghiberti 23 perspective
used his great architect
Brunelleschi 22
Donatello 1386–1466
Masaccio 1401–1428
father of modern art (reality
poverty careless about his painting)
life except his painting—
Giovanni di Bicci responsible
for him. His work never recognized
until after his death.
The Pantheon—temple
Greek philosophy—golden mean
(neither too big—or too small)
kept ousted old pope
gave money for temples for Brunelleschi
elected him Signoria
Gonfaloniere (governing body)
(pres)

Grande—nobles
    Giovanni di Bicci † 1428
       |
Cosimo (Pater Patriae)   Lorenzo
1424—first public library
  ┌─────────────────┐
Piero   Giovanni
  ┌──────────┐
Lorenzo   Giuliano
(the Magnificent)

Macchiavelli (1469–1527)
Botticelli
────────────────────

damn near broke my back
and dislocated my neck trying not to
sleep all over the filipino boy
Moved my seat when a
[illegible] left the bus—the
only empty seat so
I left mine for so the
girl could sit her kid
down and I took the
other seat. It was next to
a filipino boy and
he smelled good like
flowers.

45

good — Feb 24 / New Yorker.

I saw a lot of ~~young~~ lonely young sailors who looked too young to be so sad. they ~~looked like~~ reminded me of slender young trees, still growing & painful

— note — girl next to me for a while she was younger than I both as kid about five. That she held as if he were six months — the seats were so small & crowded especially when the people in front of you push the button for the chairs to recline I slept all over the kid next to me and the kid slept all over me. It was not exactly drafty around the windows

and made any attempt at the nook

~~pre~~ Feb 24 New-Yorker

I saw a lot of lonely young
sailors who/they looked too
young to be so sad.
They ~~looked like slender~~ reminded me of
young slender trees still
growing & painful

rode—girl next to me for a while she was
younger than I with a kid about five that
she held as if he were six months—the
seats were so small and crowded
especially when the people in front of you
push the button for the chairs to recline
I slept all over the kid next to me and
the kid slept all over me. It was really hot
except drafty around the windows
and made my throat/neck ache

Marilyn with a book about Goya, around 1953
Marilyn and Degas sculpture, Los Angeles, 1956

OTHER "RECORD" NOTEBOOK

This black notebook has a smoother cover than the preceding one. Only the first few pages have been filled; pages 3 and 4 have disappeared, because Marilyn either ripped out the sheet to write on, or did so on rereading it. It is likely that this group of notes, which is coherent and forms a certain continuity, dates from the time Marilyn started working with Lee Strasberg, around 1955. A sincere effort at introspection can be observed as the star returned to her childhood and the lifelong fears it engendered. Aunt Ida is probably Ida Martin (rather than Ida Bolender, with whom Marilyn also stayed as a child). Ida Martin was the mother of Marilyn's aunt by marriage, an evangelical Christian and strict disciplinarian who emphasized obedience and was repressive about sexual issues in general; she may also have made the twelve-year-old Norma Jeane feel guilty for an episode in which she said she had been molested.

To no longer feel ashamed of what you were, of what you desired: this was what Marilyn, who had made her childhood dream come true by becoming an actress, was now aiming for. We may also assume that she had just started psychoanalysis, as she pointed out the bent of the unconscious to forget and repress, an impulse she urged herself to struggle against by trying to reclaim memory in order to be able to accept herself fully.

She experienced work as a way of freeing herself from the constraints and shackles of the past, and these pages can be read as an outline of self-analysis, both gripping and moving.

<u>life starts from Now</u>

Ida – I have still
been obeying her –
its not only harmful
(inhibits myself,
my work, thoughts)
for me to do so
but un reality (because)

In my work – I don't
want to obey her any longer
and I can do my work as fully
as I wish since as a small child
intact first desire was to be an actress)
I have not be punished
(about page 8) and I spent years
or trying to hide it play acting until in all jobs

enjoying myself as fully
as I wish or want to
I will be as sensitive as
I am – without being ashamed of it

trust in the
faith in the simple
objects and tasks (sense
memory – outside and inside
objects)
I havent had faith in life
meaning Reality – what
ever it is or happens
There is nothing to
hold on to – but reality.
To realize the present
what ever it may be
– because thats how it
is and its much better

life starts from now

Ida—I have still
been obeying her—   (inhibits myself
it's not only harmful   inhibits my work
for me to do so   inhibits thoughts)
but unrealality because

In my work—I don't
want to obey her any longer
and I can do my work as fully
as I wish since as a small child
intact first desire was to be an actress
and I spent years
play acting until I had jobs
I have
I will not be punished
[cont. page 8]
or trying to hide it
enjoying myself as fully
as I wish or want to
I will be as sensitive as
I am—without being ashamed of it

trust in the
faith in the simple
objects and tasks—(sense
memory—outside and inside
objects)
I haven't had Faith in Life
meaning Reality—what
ever it is or happens
There is nothing to
hold on to—but reality
to realize the present
what ever it may be
—because that's how it
is and it's much better   >>>

to Know Reality (or
things as they are than
~~to know~~ not to Know
and to have few
illusions as possible—

Train my will now

>>>   to know reality (or   train my will now
things <u>as they are</u> than
~~to have~~ not to know
and to have few
illusions as possible—

working (doing) my tasks that I
have set for myself
on the stage — I will
not be punished for it
or be whipped
or " " threatened
or not be loved
or sent to hell to burn with bad people
feeling that I am also bad.
or be afraid of my genitals being
exposed known and seen —
or ashamed
or guilty of my sexual
feelings — They are reality
and I do have feeling
or colors or screaming or
very strongly sexed feeling
since a small child — (Think of
all the things I felt then

I do know ways people
act unconventually — mainly
myself — do not be afraid of
my sensitivity or to use it — (for I
can + will channel it — + crazy thoughts too
want to do my (scene
as sincerly as I exercise)
can knowing and showing
how I know it is also — no
matter — what they might
think — or judge from it

working (doing my tasks that I
have set for myself)
On the stage—I will
not be punished for it
or be whipped
or be threatened
or not be loved
or sent to hell to burn with bad people
or feeling that I am also bad.
or be afraid of my **genitals** being
or ashamed
exposed known and seen—
so what
or ashamed of my sensitive feelings—
they are reality
or colors or screaming or doing
nothing
and I do have feeling
very strongly sexed feeling
since a small child—(think of all the
things I felt then

<u>I do know</u> ways people
act unconventionally—mainly
myself—do not be afraid of
my sensitivity or to use it—for I
can & will channel it + crazy thoughts too
I want to do my scene or exercises
([illegible] idiotic as they seem)
as sincerely as ~~possible~~ I
can knowing and showing
how <u>I know</u> it is also—<u>no
matter</u>—what they might
think—or judge from it

I can and will help
my self and work on
things analitically no
matter how painful — if I
forget things (the unconcise wants to
forget — I will only try to remember)
Dicipline — Concentration

my body is my body
every part of it.

I can and will help
myself and work on
things analytically no
matter how painful—if I
forget things (the unconscious
wants to
forget—I will only try to remember)
Discipline—Concentration

my body is my body
every part of it.

12

feel what I feel.
within myself – that is,
become aware of it, trying to
also what I feel in others
not being ashamed of my
feeling, thoughts or ideas

13

realize the thing that
they are –

feel what I feel
within myself—that is trying to
become aware of it
also what I feel in others
not being ashamed of my
feeling, thoughts—or ideas

realize the thing <u>that</u>
they are—

When I start to
feel sudenly depressed
what does it come from
(in reality) trace incidents.
maybe to.
ex past time - feeling guilt?

realize all the sensitity
asspects. not being ashamed
of what ever I feel
don't dismiss
this lightly either.

not regretting saying
what I've said if it
is really true to me

even when it is not
under stood - (don't even
try to convince anyone to
much as to why - unless I
really want to - or really feel it.

tension - where do
I feel it be aware
of it where/what do I
think I comes from

conciously make effort to
relax brows
temples
are we around mouth.
cheek collapsed shoulders changing
jaws loose

make effort to be
aware - like when feeling
sick - try to stop chain reaction
before it gets started. if
if does start - don't worry
realize it be aware of it
conciously making the effort

When I start to
feel suddenly depressed
what does it come from
(in reality) trace incidents
maybe to
ex past time—feeling guilty?
realize all the sensitivity
aspects. not being ashamed
of whatever I feel
                    don't dismiss
                    this lightly either
not regretting saying
what I've said if it
is really true to me
even when it is not
understood—(don't even
try to convince anyone too
much as to why—unless I
really want to—or really feel it.

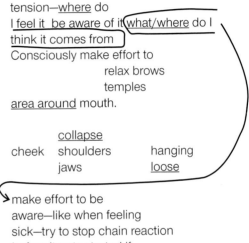

tension—where do
I feel it be aware of it what/where do I
think it comes from
Consciously make effort to
                  relax brows
                  temples
area around mouth.

                collapse
cheek   shoulders   hanging
           jaws   loose

make effort to be
aware—like when feeling
sick—try to stop chain reaction
before it gets started if
it does start—don't worry
realize it be aware of it
consciously making the effort

having a sense of myself.

having a sense of myself

Marilyn reading *To the Actor* by Michael Chekhov, New York, 1955
Marilyn writing at home, May 1953

WALDORF-ASTORIA STATIONERY

1955

Marilyn Monroe's immense popular appeal had at last been recognized by the Hollywood elite, who had gathered together at a party given in her honor by Charles Feldman, the producer of *The Seven Year Itch*, on November 6, 1954, at the Beverly Hills Romanoff. Still dissatisfied with what Hollywood had to offer, Marilyn decided to leave the West Coast for New York and set up Marilyn Monroe Productions with the photographer Milton Greene. This was a tremendous challenge to the all-powerful studios and a gesture for which she would never really be fully forgiven. From then on her life would swing between the West Coast and the East Coast, a contest between the movie-star image and the cultural and artistic self-invention that the Actors Studio and her New York acquaintances made possible. After a few weeks spent at the Gladstone Hotel, she stayed in a three-room suite on the twenty-seventh floor of the Waldorf-Astoria from April to September 1955. The following documents were written on this prestigious hotel's stationery. They include a long prose poem, the account of a nightmarish dream that is full of surprises (not least her drama teacher turning into a surgeon), thoughts and notes about what Lee Strasberg had said (she misspelled his name with a double "s") during the classes she attended at the Actors Studio, the draft of a letter to a certain "Claude," and a list of song titles. Some of these documents are discontinuous, and the links between texts, which might have been written in any order, have been left to the reader's discernment.

O sad, sweet trees —
I wish for you — rest
but you must be awake

so many

lights in the darkness
making skeletons of Buildings
and life in the streets
What was it

The things I thought about yesterday

down on the streets?

Now Seems so far away (up here) Long ago

and moon so full and dark
Its better They told me as a child what it was
for I could not guess it or understand it
now.

noises of impatience from cab drivers who always driving
must drive — Hot, dusty, icy streets so they
can eat, and perhaps save for a vacation, in which they
can drive their wives all the way across the
country to see her relatives —
the part the river made of pepsi cola — thank god for the park
yet I am not looking at these things
I'm looking for my Lover
its good they told me what
was when I was a child

then the river —
the part made of
pepsi cola —

what was that now —
Just a moment ago —
from it was mine and
now its gone — like the
swift movement of a moment
gone —
maybe I'll remember
it felt
because as though it
started to be
only — mine

Sad, sweet trees—
I wish for you—rest
but you must be wakeful

What was that now—
just a moment ago—
from it was mine and
now it's gone—like the
swift movement of a moment
gone—
maybe I'll remember
because it felt
as though it
started to be ~~wonderful~~
~~only~~ mine

Sooooo many lights in the darkness
making skeletons of buildings
and life in the streets
~~The things~~ What ~~were~~ was it I thought about yesterday
~~down~~ in the streets?
It ~~now~~ seems so far away ~~up here~~ long ago
and moon ~~so full and dark~~.
It's better ~~I earned~~ they told me as a child what it was
for I could not ~~guess it or~~ understand it now.
Noises ~~from~~ of impatience from cab drivers always driving who
must drive—hot, dusty, ~~snowing~~ icy streets so they
can eat, and perhaps save for a vacation, in which they
~~will~~ can drive their wives all the way across the
country to see her relatives.
Then the river—the part made of pepsi cola—the park—thank god for the park
Yet I am not looking at these things
I'm looking for my lover
It's good they told me what
the moon was when I was a child. >>>

That
and swells
silent ~~stirring~~ river which stirs
itself with whatever passes over it

Wind Lain, great ships ~~its~~ never unmoved
by any thing
                I love the river—

Its quite now
And the silence is alone
                thunderous
except for the rumbling of things unknown
        but   for the screems   distant drums. very present
        and   the   whispers   of things
    sharp sounds
>harp and percincing of and then suddenly hushed

to moans beyond sadness—terror beyond
fear   too
        The cry of things dim and young to be known
        The sobs of life itself   that   yet

And bear the pain & the day   You must suffer—
of newness on your limbs   to loose your dark golden
                                                                when your covering of
                                                                even dead leaves leave you

Loneliness—be still   strong and Naked—
                                                                you must be—
                                                                alive—when looking dead
                                                                straight though bent
                                                                with wind

>>> That silent ~~stirring~~ river which stirs
and swells itself with whatever passes over it
wind, rain, great ships.
I love the river—~~it is~~ never unmoored
by anything
It's quiet now
And the silence is alone
except for the thunderous rumbling of things unknown
distant drums very present
but for the **piercing** of screams
and the whispers of things
sharp sounds and then suddenly hushed
to moans beyond sadness—terror beyond
fear
The cry of things dim and **too** young **to be known yet**
The sobs of life itself

And bear the pain & the joy
of newness on your limbs

Loneliness—be still

You must suffer—
to loose your dark golden
when your covering of
even dead leaves leave you
strong and naked
you must be—
alive—when looking dead
straight though bent
with wind

make no more promises - explanations - if possible - Anne-Karen or
" " " " Recolfecting after this make no tie
commitments or engagements
myself down to save to keep
in future - able to
not being
them and mostly
avoid feeling guilty
which is now the
case

The Towers of
THE WALDORF-ASTORIA
NEW YORK
ELDORADO 5-3100

Dear Ernest

Surgeon - Strass begins
to cut me open which I dont mind since Dr. H.
has prepared me - given me anestetic
and has also dyagnosed the case and
agrees with what has to be done -
an Operation - to bring myself back to
life and to cave me of this terrible dis-ease
what ever the hell it is -

Arthur - is the only one waiting in the outer
room - worrying & hoping operation successful
for many reasons - for myself - for his play and
for himself indirectly.

Hedda - Concerned - keeps calling on phone during
operation - Norman - keeps stopping by hospital to
see if Im okay but mostly to comfort Art
who is so worried -

Milton calls from big office with lots of room
and every thing in good taste - and is conducting
business in a new way with style - and music
is playing and he is relaxed and enjoying himself even if he
is very worried at the same time - theres a camera
on his desk but he doesnt take pictures anymore except
of great paintings.

Strassberg cuts me open after Dr H. gives me

Best finest surgeon—Strasberg
~~waits~~ to cut me open which I don't mind since Dr. H
has prepared me—given me **anesthetic**
and has also diagnosed the case and
agrees with what has to be done—
an operation—to bring myself back to
life and to cure me of this terrible dis-ease
whatever the hell it is—
Arthur is the only one waiting in the outer
room—worrying and hoping operation successful
for many reasons—for myself—for his play and
for himself indirectly
Hedda—concerned—keeps calling on phone during
operation—Norman—keeps stopping by hospital to
see if I'm okay but mostly to comfort Art
who is so worried—
Milton calls from big office with lots of room
and everything in good taste—and is conducting
business in a new way with style—and music
is playing and he is relaxed and enjoying himself even if he
is very worried at the same time—there's a camera
on his desk but he doesn't take pictures anymore except
of great paintings.
Strasberg cuts me open after Dr. H gives me

>>>

Make no more promises
make no more
explanations—if possible.
Regarding Anne Karger
after this make no
commitments or tie
myself down to engagements
in future—to save
not being able to keep
them and mostly to
avoid feeling guilty
which is now the
case.

Notes:

Anne Karger was the mother of the man sometimes identified as Marilyn's first real love, Fred Karger, whom she met in 1948 when he was a (then-married) voice coach at Columbia Pictures. She stayed on good terms with Anne all her life.

Dr. H. refers to Dr. Margaret Hohenberg (see page 201).

Hedda Rosten had been a close friend of Marilyn's since 1955 and became her personal assistant for a time. Norman was Hedda's husband.

"Art" was one of the nicknames Marilyn gave to Arthur Miller.

Milton Greene took many photos of Marilyn before becoming her business partner.

for. D. H. tell about That horrible trying to
dream of the repulsive man-who is leaning to close to me in
elevator- and my panic and there my Thought with despise in
all he even looks like he has a general glasses — dot
that means I'm attracted to him

One sits here and trys in a medical way to comfort
me - everything in the room is white infact I
cant even see anyone just white objects-

They cut me open - Strassberg with Holenbergs ass.
and there is absolutly nothing there - strass berg is
deeply dis apointed but more even - academically amazed
that he had made such a mistake He thought there was going to be so much - more than
he had ever dreammed possible in almost anyone but
in stead there was absolutly nothing - devoid of
every human living feeling thing - the only thing
that came out was so finely cut sawdust - like
out of a raggady ann doll - and the sawdust spills
all over the floor & table and Dr. H. is puzzeled
because sudenly she realizess that this is a
new type case - the (puple & student - I started to write)
patient existing of complete emptyness
strassbergs dreams & hopes for theater are fallen
D. H's   " " a permant phyicatreic cure
is given up - Arthurs - is disapointed - let down &

For Dr H.
tell about that
dream of the horrible
repulsive man—who is trying to
lean too close to me in
elevator—and my panic
and then all my thought
despising him—does that mean
I'm attached
to him

>>> anesthesia and tries in a medical way to comfort
me—everything in the room is white in fact I
can't even see anyone just white objects—
they cut me open—Strasberg with Hohenberg's ass.
and there is absolutely nothing there—Strasberg is
deeply disappointed but more even—academically amazed
that he had made such a mistake. He thought there was going
to be so much—more than he had ever dreamed possible in
almost anyone but
instead there was absolutely nothing—devoid of
every human living feeling thing—the only thing
that came out was so finely cut sawdust—like
out of a raggedy ann doll—and the sawdust spills
all over the floor & table and Dr. H is puzzled
because suddenly she realizes that this is a
new type case of puple. The patient (pupil—or student—I started to write) existing
        of complete emptiness
Strasberg's dreams & hopes for theater are fallen.
Dr. H's dreams and hopes for a permanent psychiatric cure
is given up—Arthur is disappointed—let down +

He even looks
like he has
a venereal
disease.

why did it to
mean so much all that
me when after all that
crying sobbing on
stage — He said when
I was kind of

The Towers of
THE WALDORF-ASTORIA
NEW YORK
ELDORADO 5-3100

I want you all to know
that this exercise went on for
½ hr. and her concentration did
not give way or slip once — and there
will be very few times ever on the
stage where it will be
neccesary to keep
such a concentration
for one half hour —
straight.

Dear Art,

Don't overwork — Keep well

reaction — I'm always afraid when so one praises me its even
worse in its own peculiar way (the way that) makes me
suffer with such misgivings) that the whole thing is an
accident even probably it wasn't me at all

everyone has violence in themselves
I am violent —

time with it
away either and not waste
dea.. with fear no running
proper channels — which is (means)
it from fear into the
your sensitivity to turn
to be done — to deal with
Remember — technical things
that fear and fear alone
from just run and acting only
into just fear and acting only
effects (turning your fear against yourself)
able to handle it
not get rid of it
without dangerous

most people in this country
take it the oppisite way you
do and thats why (some people)
you know admire you — just for
that

but your sensitivity
would not be the same
if you didnt have these
fearful misgivings — which
from your experiens (past) you
reacted but tecnically you will be

Why did it
mean so much to
me when after all that
crying sobbing on
stage—he said when
I was kind of

I want you all to know
that this exercise went on for
½ hour and her concentration did not
give way or slip once—and Marilyn there
will be very few times ever on the
stage where it will be
necessary to keep
such a concentration
for one half hour
straight.

~~Dear Art,~~
~~Don't overwork—keep well~~

reaction (—I'm always afraid when someone praises me it's even
worse in its own peculiar way in that particular way it makes me
suffer with such misgivings)—that the whole thing is an
accident even probably it wasn't me at all

everyone has violence in themselves. I am violent.

most people in this country
take it the opposite way you
do and that's why (partly I put that in) some people
you know admire you—just for
that

but your sensitivity
would not be the same
if you didn't have these
fearful misgivings?—which
from your experience (past) you've reacted but
technically you will be
able to handle it
not get rid of it
without dangerous effects

whole thing backwards
(turning your fear against yourself)
into just fear and acting only
from that—fear and fear alone
Remember—technical things can
to be done—to deal with
your sensitivity to turn
it from fear into the
proper channels—which is (means)
dealing with fear, not running
away either and not waste
time with it.

not geared to Remember— Your own (it doesn't feel like it)
lonely little girl You but have any help you want— personally— or in your
anymore much talent   work— or anything else you want—
                        There are technical ways to go about it
          much ability   or problems— figure out if anything tec- can be done
                        about it because there are people to help you— gladly— who
And much too much sensitivity to invert yourself   more than most
                                                    they want to
    out of fear— not going to class—   help
or to do things like being afraid to come to
class or to get up— remember there is nothing you
                    Luck— nothing to be self conscious about
                    yourself— you have everything but the discipline
                    and technich which you are learning & seeking
                    where-ever you well   &sure

like Susie— where you and there is a kind of light about
you— no acting can give you this quality.   oh your own was or
                                            after all nothing was
                                            is being given to you
                                            you have had none of this
                                            worth-thrown your way
the sensitivity is so strong— much deeper and stronger than that
                                            your seeked it
of susies   full and so   it didn't seek you
        In fact the sensitivity is so strong   it is dangerous
                    could be   most cases there is not the
                                        emotional
because— the emotions & rule everything.
he feels
I will be able for my first part its really to a tremendous part
which is rare— like in the case of susie   Her background different
                            surprisingly   disciplined developed she posses so you
exposure —embarrassing
    The best actors Ouise had it that sometimes she wouldn't play not that
she couldn't but didn't wish to expose herself in her then present state

my fear is not illogical only its illogical at this time— don't work out
on it— tecnical devises will help my concentration.
        come   Remember the
            the difficulties & fear is always there and will be
to overn-   But there is something you can do about it
in your case
tecnically   which by only making the effort by carrying out the tec-
            (putting them together— there is a sciene.)
-nical exercises.

Strasberg
        (Him he said)
It makes me feel badly (and sadly) for you that you do
practically things out of fear
    You must start to do things out of strength—
(my aunt)
where do I get the strength)— he said— by not looking for strength
but only looking & seeking tecnical ways and means.

Remember you(r) can sitting on top of the world (it doesn't feel like it).
You can have any help you want personally—or in your
work—or anything else you want—
There are technical ways to go about it
or problems—figure out if anything tec. can be done
about it because there are people to help you—<u>gladly</u>—you
more than most they want to help
Remember there is nothing you
lack—nothing to be self conscious about
yourself—you have everything but the discipline
and technique which you are learning & seeking
on your own—
after all nothing was or
is being given to you—
you have had none of this
work thrown your way
you **sought** it
—it didn't seek you

Not a scared
lonely little girl
anymore

Too much talent
Too much ability and
and much too much sensitivity to invert yourself
out of fear—not come to class—
or to do things like being afraid to come to
class or to get up.

Like Susie—where you are wherever you walk there is a kind of light about
you—no acting can give you this quality.
The sensitivity is so strong—much deeper and stronger than that
of Susie's.
In fact the sensitivity is so full and so strong it is dangerous
because the emotions can & do rule everything—most cases there is not the emotional.
He feels I will be able for my first part to really be a tremendous part
which is rare—like in the case of Susie. Her background different
surprisingly discipline (self-developed) she possessed so young.
<u>Exposure</u>—embarrassing.
The best actors. Duse had it that sometimes she wouldn't play (not that
she couldn't but didn't wish to expose herself in her then present state

my fear is not illogical only it's illogical at this time—don't work out
of it—technical devices will help my concentration.

to overcome the difficulties Remember the fear is always there and will be
in your case. But there is something you can do about it
<u>technically</u> which by <u>only</u> making the effort, by carrying out the
technical exercises (putting them together—there is a scene)

Strasberg
it makes me (him he said) feel badly (and sadly) for you that you do
~~practically every~~ things out of fear
You must start to do things out of strength—
(my question: where do I get the strength)—he said—by not looking for strength
but only looking & seeking <u>technical</u> ways and means

Note: Susie was the nickname of Lee and Paula Strasberg's daughter, born in 1938.
At the time she knew Marilyn, she had started a career as a theater actress and also
attended the Actors Studio.

Please don't talk about me when I'm gone

You're an old smoothie

Body and Soul

Who's Sorry Now

easy living
when I'm not near the Boy I love 259

While we're young 262

I know where I'm going and who's going with me?

I cried for you

You do something

the gentleman is a dope

I'll never be the same

He's funny that way

too Marvelous for words

Don't worry about me   Have you ever
what is There to say   been lonely
But not for me   I've got under my
Easy to Love   skin

Please don't talk about me when I'm gone

You're an old smoothie

Body and soul?

Who's sorry now

Easy living

When I'm not near the boy I Love   259

While we're young   262

I know where I'm going and who's going with me?

I cried for you

You do something

The gentleman is a dope

I'll never be the same

He's funny that way

too marvelous for words

Don't worry about me

What is there to say

But not for me

Easy to love

Have you ever been lonely

I've got you under my skin

Note: This is a set of song titles. Numbers 259 and 262 are the corresponding numbers to a fake book, or an anthology of lyrics and chord progressions from which musicians could improvise. It is not known why Marilyn made this list; possibly they were songs she wished to perform.

Dear Claude —

That's right — I know exactly what I'm doing and I know
I've just written — Dear Claude — Meanwhile besides
the way of a country man

to hunt his training stuff

his progress how he is trying
in fact he is surprised
Write to him —

I don't want to stop ... for you.
I'm knowing

at course it's simple
to be a member of the
Mr. Johnson Club because

probably probably stress as strong
got kicked out of the Club probably older
for builder Dr. Jefferson

if you haven't come back from
why don't you

your needed here
Hope you'll come to

it's true that I ask this question
is this true that I was a member
am I under the cool stand improve one at a
as a member there rules
but then how is
of Boodles Club one to know gone

also a new Mr. Johnson it's easier ever to
member at the Mr. Johnson be a member of the Mr. Club
where Go

P.S. In a few short days I'm ghastly you
even under — to remind you — sometimes

This might serve as the
watchword for someweekend
don't you think

do you think I've gone too far

Re- Reminder

84 Remsen St.
Brooklyn!

Dear Claude Claude,
That's right—I know exactly what I'm doing and I
know ~~mean~~
I've just written ~~Dear~~ Claude, Claude—
~~it's because~~ meanwhile besides
"The way of a country man is hard, his training
strict, his progress slow, his disappointments
many." If in fact he is to ~~survive~~ succeed he must
~~should~~ "give it up." Are you prepared? I am
interested only per one "borderline" to the other.
in knowing from one of course it's ~~easier~~ simpler
to be a member of the Mr. Johnson club because
for when one could probably get kicked out of
the club for stress, ~~or~~ strain or **exertion** as
probably forbidden—
but then how is one to know
since there are no rules
I ask this question as a member of good standing
of Borderline Anonymous also as a newly
chartered member of the Mr. Johnson club.
It's easier even to be a member of the M.J. Club
where for any kind of exertion, stress or strain
you're kicked out.
Is it/this true that I am under the right impression
My love to Hedda and Patty and Candy and
Bammoo. Come back if you haven't come back
from Port Jefferson yet (hope you've)—why
don't you.
You're needed here.
looking forward to seeing you all
Love
Marilyn

P.S. In a few short days I'm sending you
a reminder—to remind you ~~of something~~
of me mostly

This might ~~very well~~ serve as
(the)/(a) possible watchword for some
other weekend don't you think
or
do you think I've gone too far

Re—reminder [drawing of envelope]

84 Remsen St.
Brooklyn
Heights

Notes:
Marilyn nicknamed her friend Norman Rosten "Claude"
because he looked so much like the actor Claude Rains.
He and his wife, Hedda, had a daughter called Patricia
(Patty). At this time they lived in Brooklyn, at 84 Remsen
Street.

Bam-Moo and Candy were the names of the Rostens'
dog and cat.

The Mr. Johnson club was invented by Norman Rosten
and Marilyn; the name refers to Rosten's play *Mister
Johnson*, based on Joyce Cary's novel, which embodied
for Marilyn the spirit of innocence destroyed by cynicism
and greed.

On the balcony of the Ambassador Hotel, New York, 1955
Marilyn Monroe with Truman Capote, New York, 1955

ITALIAN AGENDA

1955 or 1956

In an Italian diary engraved in green, Marilyn Monroe wrote down thoughts in free association in continuation of a kind of self-analysis she had begun to practice in the "Record" notebook (she noticed with amusement her own Freudian slip when she wrote the first three letters of the name "Buddy" as "Bad"). It isn't really known who the woman with big breasts was: perhaps her analyst, Dr. Hohenberg (mentioned on another page)? A salaried member of her circle? In any case, Marilyn remembered two traumatic moments: as a lonely child, when, despite the lies she told, a teacher was one of the only people who seemed to understand her; and an incident of sexual abuse for which Ida Martin, her foster mother, seemed to have taken her to task rather than consoling or helping her. It is likely that these pages correspond to work on repressed memory undertaken as part of her analysis with Dr. Hohenberg, which she started in February 1955. Her relationship with her third husband, Arthur Miller, seemed to be idyllic still, propelled as it was by strong desire and absolute confidence: there is no trace of either doubt or crisis.

She also evoked her relationship to fear, which she seemed to need to draw on for her acting but which terrorized her as well. The Peter whom she mentions twice as a source of fear and threat could well be Peter Lawford, whom she knew in the early 1950s, although it is not known with what degree of intimacy. Lawford later became John Kennedy's brother-in-law upon his marriage to Patricia Kennedy. Some years later Marilyn often saw the Lawford couple and visited their Santa Monica beach house several times.

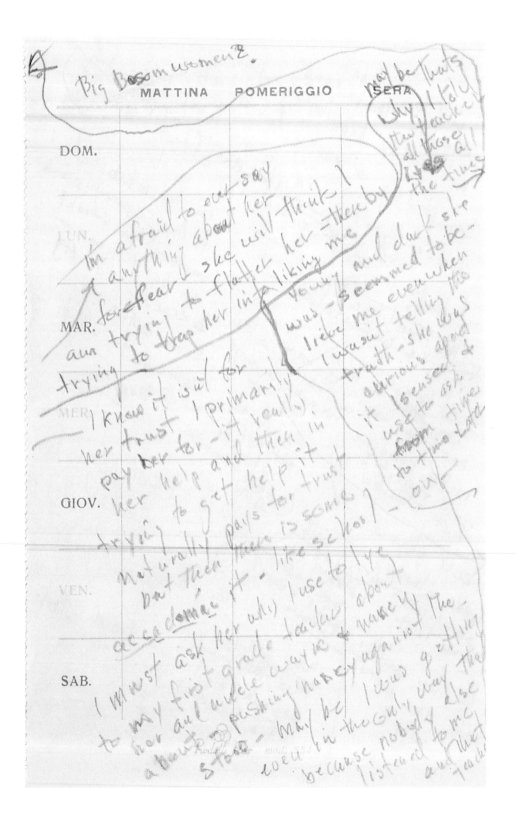

Big Bosom women 2.

	MATTINA	POMERIGGIO	SERA

DOM.

LUN.

MAR.

MER.

GIOV.

VEN.

SAB.

I'm afraid to even say anything about her for fear she will think I am trying to flatter her - thereby trying to trap her into liking me

young and dark she was - seemed to be - like me even when I wasn't telling the truth - she was curious about it seemed + used to ask from time to time to find out

maybe that's why I told Peacock all those all the times

I know it is n't for her trust I primarily pay her for - it really is her help and then in trying to get help it naturally pays for trust but then there is some academic it - like school

I must ask her why I use to lye to my first grade teacher about her and uncle wayne + nancy the about pushing money against the store - maybe I used getting even in the only way because nobody else listened to me and they teach

because she interested
seemed so interested
in them and seemed
to talk to me & like me
maybe I didn't want
her to treat me like aunt Ida
did –

MATTINA   POMERIGGIO   SERA

DOM.

LUN.

MAR.

MER.

GIOV.

VEN.

SAB.

Prodotti Flex   mod. 854

Big Bosom Women?

I'm afraid to ever say
anything about her
for fear she will think I
am trying to flatter her—thereby
trying to trap her into liking me,

I know it isn't for
her trust I primarily
pay her for—it really **is**
her help and then in
trying to get help it
naturally pays for trust
but then there is some
<u>academic</u> **in** it—like school—
I must ask her why I use**d** to lie
to my first grade teacher about
her and uncle wayne & nancy
about pushing nancy against the
stove—maybe I was getting
even in the only way that
because nobody else
listened to me
and that
teacher

Maybe that's
why I told
the teacher
all those
lies all
the time

Young and dark she
was—seemed to be-
lieve me even when
I wasn't telling the
truth—she was
curious about
it I sensed &
use**d** to ask
from time
to time later
on—

because she
seemed so interested
in them and seemed
to talk to me & like me
maybe I didn't want
her to treat me like Aunt Ida
did—

Note: Ida Bolender and her husband, Albert Wayne,
cared for Norma Jeane at their home in Hawthorne from
June 1926, shortly after her birth, and she stayed with
them until she was seven. The child called Ida Wayne's
husband "Daddy" despite the fact that Ida Bolender
would have preferred her to call him "Uncle Wayne."
The Bolenders adopted two children: Nancy, who was
five years younger, and Lester, who was the same age
as Marilyn.

I am so concerned about protecting Arthur - and he is the (I am not only practically) I love him - and he is the only person - human being I have known that I could love not as a man to which I am attracted to practically out of my senses about - but he the only person - a another human being that I Trust as much as myself - because when I do Trust my-self - I do fully and certainly and do about him also -

Peter wants - where as Peter wants to be a woman - and I think I would like to be me -

also I trust Dr H. though in a different way since I have to pay her However

in fact now I think I know why he's been here so long because I have a need to be frighten - and nothing really in my person and dealings have been frightening me - except times with him - I felt very uneasy at different I was afraid of him - to because I believe him to be homosexual - not in the real way I know + respect and admire talent and would I feel feels be jealous of me because I wouldn't really want to be me

why is it I have a feeling - things are - but
not really happening - for which
I am playing a part - in as much as I know - what I knew - premeditated - except)
I feel guilty, in as much - in spite its effect -
what I am saying and the

the feeling of violence
we had lately

about being afraid of
of them - or me etc. look in
harm me - power me
maybe someone why - strange
will read it?
I don't think so
his eyes - strange
behaviors

i'm too inhibited
to feel spontaneous
because I'm afraid
to be I mean
because I doubt
know what will
come out - what
will happen

even gas
and maybe
stomahole
(afraid to write
fart)

I was physically sure
some was wrong with
me. There
in other words
I'm the worst
why?
afraid to
say above
but I know
whether

and I will be
humiliated and
feel lower than
anything or anyone

Why do I feel
this torture?
or why do I feel Less
of a human being than other
I always so of felt in
a way that I'm
sub-human
why

I am so concerned
about protecting Arthur
I love him—and he is the
only person—human being I have
ever known that I could love not only
as a man to which I am attracted to practically
out of my senses about—but he **is** the only
person—as another human being that I trust as
much as myself—because when I do trust myself (about certain things) I do <u>fully</u>, and I
do about him also—

also I trust Dr. H.
though in a different
way since I have to pay
her for it however

whereas Peter wants
to be a woman—and
would like to be me—I think

in fact now I think I know
why he's been here so long
because I have a need to
be frighten—and nothing really
in my personal relationships (and dealings) lately
have been frightening me—except
for him—I felt very uneasy at different
times with him—the real reason
I was afraid of him—is because I believe
him to be homosexual—not in the
way I love & respect and admire **Jack**
who I feel feels I have talent
and wouldn't be jealous
of me because I wouldn't
really want to
be me

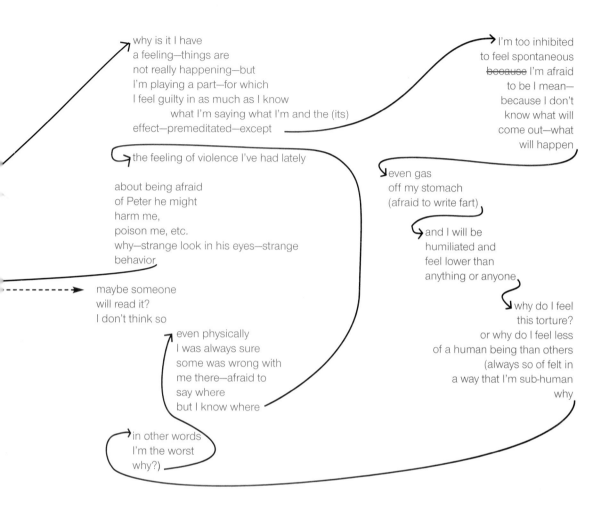

why is it I have
a feeling—things are
not really happening—but
I'm playing a part—for which
I feel guilty in as much as I know
what I'm saying what I'm and the (its)
effect—premeditated—except

I'm too inhibited
to feel spontaneous
~~because~~ I'm afraid
to be I mean—
because I don't
know what will
come out—what
will happen

the feeling of violence I've had lately

about being afraid
of Peter he might
harm me,
poison me, etc.
why—strange look in his eyes—strange
behavior

even gas
off my stomach
(afraid to write fart)

and I will be
humiliated and
feel lower than
anything or anyone

maybe someone
will read it?
I don't think so

even physically
I was always sure
some was wrong with
me there—afraid to
say where
but I know where

why do I feel
this torture?
or why do I feel less
of a human being than others
(always so of felt in
a way that I'm sub-human
why

in other words
I'm the worst
why?)

Notes:
The Peter who is mentioned is possibly the British-born actor Peter Lawford, a friend of Marilyn's and brother-in-law to the Kennedys through his marriage to Pat, the president's sister.

If indeed it is the name "Jack" that is written (the writing is difficult to decipher), it could refer to Jack Cole, a dancer friend of Marilyn's who coached her on the films *Gentlemen Prefer Blondes* and *There's No Business Like Show Business*.

I'm finding that sincerity (I'd like
and trying to be as simple or direct as (possible)
is often taken for sheer stupidity

but since it is not a sincere
world — (its very probable that being sincere is stupid)
One probably is stupid to
be sincere since its in this world
and know other world that we know
for sure we exist — meaning that —
(Since reality exist it should be, must be dealt)
there is reality to deal with

with) — since should be met and delt with

I'm ~~Will~~ — I'm not permitted

I'm
Edward &
Merrows show)

Problems
nervousness
humanness
blunders
mistakes
and my own
thoughts

This of course   (a few drinks
is taken for   to many — occaue(ly)
over drinking —   meaning maybe I
                        didnt have time to
and the more it   eat during day
I think of   and since socially
the more I   liqueur is accepted
realise there   possibly previously
are no answers   and knowly — I might
life is to be   feel a need to relax
                        with a few glasses of sherry
2   that might need quickly

That perhaps
I would have
not enjoyed
being too tired

and make
me suddenly
gay and respon-
sive to things
and people
around me

and since it is comparitvely
so short - (maybe too short - maybe too long -
for sure
the only thing I know, it isn't easy

wonderment

fear

"now that I want to live
and I feel suddenly not old
not concerned about previous
Things except to protect
myself - my life - and
desperately (pray) tell
the universe
I trust it

the wondering of something
ask it questions -
the unbelievableness of the activity
if it happened

about not
getting the D.
off - after four
days

slip in
your lines?

or the pleading & promising &
of any thing - reasoning -
which is more conventional,
I started to write Dad
after Buddy   instead   with fear
of Buddy
Because A.L. punished me
and whipped me - "the bad part
of my body she said -
must never touch myself
there or let any one
wash @ both - water running from it)

out the medical fear
of any part of my to
body (there - fear
touch my own body

I'm finding that sincerity
and ~~trying~~ to be ~~as~~ simple or direct as (possible) I'd like
is often taken for sheer <u>stupidity</u>
but since it is not a sincere world—
          it's very probable that being sincere is stupid.
One probably is stupid to
be sincere since it's in this world
and no other world that we know
for sure we exist—meaning that—
(since reality exists it ~~should be must be dealt~~ should be met and dealt with)
since there is reality to deal with

problems
nervousness
humanness
blunders
mistakes
and my own
thoughts

I'm ~~not~~ M.M.—I'm not permitted ~~to be~~
Edward R. Murrow's show

this of course
is taken for
over-drinking

and the more
I think of
it the more
I realize there
are no answers
life is to be
lived

(a few drinks
too many—**occasionally**)
meaning maybe I
didn't have time to
eat during day
and since socially
liquor is accepted
and possibly previously
hurrying—I might
feel a need to relax
with a few glasses of sherry
that might react too quickly

that perhaps
I would have
not enjoyed
being too tired
and make
me suddenly
gay and respon-
sive to things
and people
around me

and since it is comparatively
so short—(maybe too short—maybe too long—
the only thing I know for sure, it isn't easy

now that I want to live
and I feel suddenly ~~very young~~ not old
not concerned about previous
things except to protect
myself—my life—and to
desperately (pray) tell
the universe
I trust it

fear
wonderment
the wondering of something
ask it questions—
the unbelievableness of the actuality
if it happened.

or the pleading & promising
of anything—reasoning—
which is more conventional

slip in writing?)

(I started to write Bad
instead of Buddy—

after Buddy

about not
getting the D.
out—after four
days

because A.I. punished me
with fear and whipped me—
"the bad part of my body" she said—
must never touch myself
there or let anyone—
wash cloth—water running from it

and the immediate fear
of any part of my
body there—fear to
touch my own body

Notes:
Marilyn was a guest on Edward R. Murrow's very popular TV show *Person to Person* on April 8, 1955.

A.I. was probably Aunt Ida, that is, Ida Martin, the other Aunt Ida (the first being Ida Bolender), a great-aunt with whom Marilyn lived from November 1937 to August 1938 in Compton, California.

In the spring of 1938, Marilyn may have suffered a sexual assault by one of her fellow boarders, who could be the Buddy mentioned here.

The "D." may be short for either "doctor" or "demon."

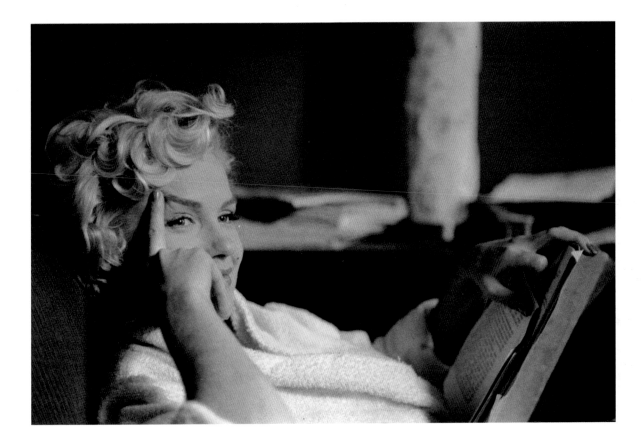

In a bookstore in Los Angeles, February 1953
On the set of *The Seven Year Itch*, 1954

PARKSIDE HOUSE STATIONERY

1956

Soon after their wedding on June 29, 1956, Marilyn and Arthur Miller went to London, where the film *The Prince and the Showgirl*, produced by Marilyn Monroe Productions, was to be shot. Laurence Olivier directed the film and played the male lead. The relationship between the two actors was difficult: Olivier was disdainful and haughty toward Marilyn.

The couple arrived in London on July 14 and stayed at Parkside House, a luxurious manor house in Egham, Surrey, near London. Everything should have been idyllic.

However, one day Marilyn found her husband's open diary and discovered that the playwright was disappointed in her, that he was sometimes ashamed of her in front of his intellectual peers, and that he had doubts about their marriage. Marilyn was extremely upset and felt betrayed.

Did she write these few poems and odd texts on Parkside House stationery before or after her discovery? In either case, their tone is mournful. They are pessimistic about love and love's possibilities as well as the inevitable passage of time.

The filming was difficult. Marilyn's acting coach Paula Strasberg was called in to help, as was Dr. Margaret Hohenberg, her New York analyst. On October 29, Marilyn Monroe was introduced to Queen Elizabeth II during a ceremony, and she went back to the United States on November 20.

The portrait on page 121 is possibly of Laurence Olivier.

my love sleeps besides me —

In the faint light — I see his ~~the~~ manly jaw

give ~~a~~ way — and the mouth of his

boyhood returns

with a softnes softer

its sensitivness ~~that~~ trembling

in stillness

his eyes must have look out

wonderously from the cave of the little

boy — when the things he did not understand

he forgot

but will he look like this when he's dead

oh unbearable fact inevitable

yet sooner would I rather his love die

than him?

my love sleeps besides me—
in the faint light—I see his manly jaw
give ~~away~~—and the mouth of his
boyhood returns
with a softness softer
its sensitiveness ~~that~~ trembling
in stillness
his eyes must have look out
wonderously from the cave of the little
boy—when the things he did not understand—
he forgot
but will he look like this when he is dead
oh unbearable fact inevitable
yet sooner would I rather his love die
than/or him?

>>>

the pain of his longing when he looks
at another—
   like an unfulfilment since the day
he was born.

and I in merciless pain
and with his pain of longing—
~~when he looks~~ at and loves another

like an unfulfilment of ~~since~~ the day
he was born—
we must endure
I more sadly because I can feel no joy

>>>

the pain of his longing when he looks
at another—
like an unfulfillment since the day
he was born.

And I in merciless pain
and with his pain of Longing—
when he looks at and loves another
like an unfulfillment of ~~since~~ the day
he was born—
we must endure
I more sadly because I can feel no joy

Silence, ~~why don't~~ aren't ~~your soothe~~ still soothe me
you~~r~~ ~~drums~~ sounds stillness hurt my ~~ears~~ head and
pirce ears with ~~sounds~~ unbearable— durable
~~Jais~~ my head with the stillness of

on the screen of pitch blackness
reapears—
Comes the shapes of monsters ~~who are~~
my most steadfast Companions—

My blood ~~is~~ throbing with unrest
turns it route in an ~~opposite~~ other direction

and the ~~white~~ world is sleeping—
ah peace I need you — even a
peaceful monster.

>>>

oh silence ~~why don't/aren't you still soothe me~~
you ~~sounds drums~~ stillness hurt my ~~ears~~ head—and
pierce ears
jars my head with the stillness of
sounds unbearable/durable—
on the screen of pitch blackness
comes/reappears the shapes of monsters ~~who are~~
my most steadfast companions—
my blood ~~is~~ throbbing with unrest
turns it route in ~~the opposite~~ another direction
and the ~~whole~~ world is sleeping
ah peace I need you—even a
peaceful monster.

PARKSIDE HOUSE,
ENGLEFIELD GREEN,
SURREY.

EGHAM 800.

To have your heart is
the only happy proud thing (that ever belonged
to me) possession (possesion) are ever
possesed So

Thing that ever completly

happen to me

521 Wissett

To have your heart is
the only completely happy proud ~~possession~~ thing (that ever belonged
to me) I've ever possessed so

thing that ever completely
happen to me

Note: Wissett is a village in Suffolk. It is not known what the
number refers to; possibly it is a phone number.

I guess I have always been deeply terrified ~~it~~ to really be some ones wife

Since I know from life one cannot love another, ever, really,

I guess I have always been
deeply terrified ~~at~~ to really be someone's
wife
    since I know from life
one cannot love another,
ever, really.

It is not ~~to be~~ for granted
~~sir~~ ~~lifeless~~ ~~that the~~ old woman hides
from her glass ~~staring~~ ~~by dust~~ —The one she polishes
so it won't be dust —
see her toothless gasp and ~~sometimes to~~ ~~if perhaps~~ she ~~smiles~~ gently
~~her~~ ~~you only~~ she remembers —
~~tired of youth~~ pain,
her pale ~~and~~ chiton dress
that she wore on a windy
afternoon when she walked
where no one had ever been
her ~~cleur eyed~~ clear eyed baby who
lived to die —The womens ~~Years hung~~ ~~th. hong~~
~~at~~ left. the woman ~~stirs~~ of stars in space

it is not to be for granted
~~in life less that~~ the old woman hides—
from her ~~mirror~~ glass—the one she polishes so it won't be dusty—
      daring sometimes ~~that to~~
to see her toothless gasp and if she perhaps very gently smiles
~~years only~~ she remembers—
her ~~life or imagined youth~~ pain
her pale chiffon dress
that she wore on a windy
afternoon when she walked
where no one had ever been
her ~~blue-eyed~~ clear eyed baby who
lived to die—the woman's ~~youth~~ years have
~~not~~ left. The woman **stares** & **stares** in space

where his eyes rest with pleasure - I
want to still be - but time has changed
the hold of that glance -

     alas how will I cope when I am
even less youthful -

I seek joy but it is clothed

with pain -
    ~~have.~~ take heart
    ~~Courage~~ - ~~to be~~ brave as in my youth
sleep and rest my heavy head
on ~~His~~ breast - ~~because~~ for still my love
sleeps beside me.

where his eyes rest with pleasure—I
want to still be—but time has changed
the hold of that glance.

  Alas how will I cope when I am
even less youthful—

I seek joy but ~~you are~~ it is clothed
with pain—
~~have courage   to be brave~~ take heart as in my youth
sleep and rest my heavy head
on ~~your~~ his breast ~~because~~ for still my love
sleeps beside me.

Marilyn reading Whitman's *Leaves of Grass*, 1951
Marilyn reading Arthur Miller's *Death of a Salesman*, 1952

ROXBURY NOTES
1958

In the summer of 1957, Marilyn and Arthur Miller bought
a house in Roxbury, Connecticut, where Arthur had already
lived with his first wife. They initially considered having the
house demolished in order to have a new one built by
Frank Lloyd Wright, with a swimming pool, a home cinema,
a theater, and a big office for Arthur, but the project turned out to
be too expensive and they contented themselves
with renovating the property.

Marilyn probably wrote these few pages in the spring of 1958,
and their tone is particularly disenchanted. The couple stayed a
long time in the country, but, loveless now, their home seemed
empty. Arthur worked with little success on the screen
adaptation of his own short story *The Misfits*, and Marilyn
quickly got bored with her role of housewife. Even the arrival of
spring and leaves on the trees were no longer any solace, since
they reminded her of failed attempts at motherhood,
the lack of a child she had hoped for. At this time she would
look closely at her own face in a magnifying glass and observe
the effects of passing time.

Since the "other" (the beloved) was unattainable, she resigned
herself "to love bravely" and accept what she could not alter.
Here we can sense a tortured soul who still wanted to believe in
the possibility of profound connection, even as the relationship
grew more strained and distant.

starting tomorrow - I will take
care of myself for that's
all I really have and as I
see it now have ever had.
Roxbury - I've tried to imagine
spring all winter - it's here and
I still feel hopeless. I think
I hate it here because there
is no love here anymore. I
regret the effort I desperately made
here. I tried to fight what with
my being I knew was true
that due to pressures is going to sound like a telegram that come
in my work (it's funny I've always
accepted even the worst - tried to oppose it
if it meant jeopardizing my work)
he could not endure he is not whole, can't
felt (sincerely, which I am surely) that
what I could endure helped both
of us in a 2nd material way for which
means so much more to him
than me ever. - I have seen
what he intends me to see and
I am strangely calm while I catch
my breath. Is a good saying we not
so funny - what it stands for your pain
"If I had my life to live over I'd
live over a salon" Those tender green
leaves on these one hundred & seventy five
year old maples that I see (
) what was I looking at? Its life
having a child when one is ninety.
I don't want any children because I only
could trust every delicate and
indelicate feeling of my child with
myself in every accident (sounds like
an identification card) there is no one
I trust I mean if anything would happen bless myself at this moment
clearly spring the green is
too sharp though the delicacy in its form is

starting tomorrow I will take care of myself for that's all I really have and as I see it now have ever had. Roxbury—I've tried to imagine spring all winter—it's here and I still feel hopeless. I think I hate it here because there is no love here anymore. I regret the effort I desperately made here. I tried to fight what with my being I knew was true ~~that~~ due to pressure (it's going to sound like a telegram) that have come in my work (it's funny I've always accepted even the worst—tried to oppose it if it meant jeopardizing my work) he could not endure (he is from another land) though I felt (innocently, which I am <u>not</u>) that what I could endure helped both of us and in a material way ~~also~~ which means so much more to him than me even. I have seen what he intends me to see and I am strangely calm while I catch my breath. It's a good saying the not so funny—what it stands for though—pain "If I had my life to live over I'd live over a saloon"

Those tender green leaves on these one hundred & seventy five year old maples that I see (~~I wondered several what my senses felt~~ what was I looking at). It's like having a child when one is ninety. ~~I don't want any children because I only could trust every delicate and indelicate feeling of my child with myself in case of accident (sounds like an identification card)~~ there is no one I trust. I mean if anything would happen Blessed thought at this moment. In every spring the green is too sharp—though the delicacy in their form is

>>>

Note: The quote is from W. C. Fields.

sweet and uncertain th~~ere~~ – it
puts up a good strugle in the wind
trembling ~~all~~ the while. those leaves
will collapse, expand in the sun
and each rain drop they will resist
even when their batterd and ripped.
I think I am very lonely – my
mind jumps. I see myself in the
mirror now, brow ~~furrowed~~ – if
I lean close I see / what I dont
want to know – tension, sadness,
disappointment, my ~~~~ eyes dulled, cheeks
flushed with capilaries that look like
rivers on maps – hair lying like snakes.
the mouth makes me the sadest
next to my dead eyes. there is
a dark line between the lips
in the outline of several broken waves
in a turbulent storm – It says
dont kiss me, dont fool me I'm
a dancer who cannot dance

When one wants to stay alone as
My love (arthur) indicates the other must
stay apart

>>>

sweet and uncertain ~~though~~ it puts up a good struggle in the wind ~~though~~ trembling all the while. Those leaves will relax, expand in the sun and each raindrop they will resist even when **they're** battered and ripped. I think I am very lonely—my mind jumps. I see myself in the mirror now, brow furrowed— if I lean close I'll see—what I don't want to know—tension, sadness, disappointment, my ~~blue~~ eyes dulled, cheeks flushed with capillaries that look like rivers on maps—hair lying like snakes. The mouth makes me the saddest, next to my dead eyes. There is a dark line between the lips in the outline of several [illegible] waves in a turbulent storm—it says don't kiss me, don't fool me I'm a dancer who cannot dance.

When one wants to stay alone as my love (Arthur) indicates the other must stay apart.

>>>

re-relationships–

(Everyone's Childhood plays itself
out)

No wonder no one knows the
other or can completely understand
By this I don't know if I'm just giving
up with this conclusion or resigning myself or maybe
for the first time connecting with
reality –)

how do we know the pain of
another's earlier years, let alone
all that he drags with him since
along the way best a lot of lea-way is needed
for the other yet how much is
unhealthy for one to bear

I think to love bravely is the
best and accept – as much as
one can bear

>>>   re—relationships

Everyone's childhood <u>plays</u> itself out
No wonder no one knows the other or can completely understand.
By this I don't know if I'm just giving up with this conclusion or resigning
myself—or maybe for the first time connecting with reality—

how do we know the pain of another's earlier years let alone
all that he drags with him since along the way at best a lot of lee-way is
needed for the other—yet how <u>much</u> is <u>unhealthy</u> for one to bear.

I think to love bravely is the best and accept—as much as one can bear

Marilyn reading a script, Hotel Bel-Air, Los Angeles, 1952
Marilyn on her bed, Hollywood, 1962

livewire

49¢ WIDE RULED   NUMBER LW-49

RED LIVEWIRE NOTEBOOK

1958

In the spring of 1958, Marilyn had had enough of her dull country life. She wanted to start working again and was studying proposals from her agent and Fox, among which was an adaptation of Faulkner's *The Sound and the Fury,* when, out of the blue, Billy Wilder sent her a two-page summary of an old German farce he was working on, *Some Like It Hot.* On July 8 she arrived in Los Angeles for the shooting.

Marilyn used only five pages of this big red spiral notebook. It can be dated from the summer of 1958, as it includes two lines of dialogue from *Some Like It Hot* (pages 140 and 142). Why these two lines? (One might be self-referential; Marilyn was born in June just like the character of Sugar Kane.) What do they reveal about Marilyn's musings?

Another possibility presents itself: that the pencil notes were written before the ones in blue ballpoint pen. In that case, "after one year of analysis" (page 138) would refer to 1956 (she started her analysis with Dr. Hohenberg in 1955), with a hint of irony as to the result, as revealed in a short four-line poem expressing despair in the form of a cry for help: the desire to die rather than live.

I left my home of green rough wood.
a blue velvet couch I dream till now
a shiny dark bush just left of the door.
down the walk clickity clack as my doll
in her carriage went over the cracks "We'll
go far away"

look—

we left the meadows are reaching—they're touching the sky
We'll leave our outlines against the crushed grass
it will die sooner because we were there—will something
else grow? and white clouds from us
old man shapes to anything dogs with ears flying

Don't cry my doll don't cry
I hold you and rock you to sleep
hush hush I was only pretending now, that I'm
not your mother who died.

I shall feed you from the shiny dark bush
just left of the door

I left my home of green rough wood—
a blue velvet couch I dream till now
a shiny dark bush just left of the door.
[Illegible] down the walk clickity clack as my doll
in her carriage went over the cracks—"We'll go far away"

The meadows are huge the earth (will be) hard
on my back. The grass ~~surged~~ touched
the blue and still white clouds changing from an
old man shapes to a smiling dog with ears flying

Look—
The meadows are reaching—they're touching the sky
~~We'll leave~~ We left our outlines against/on the crushed grass.
It will die sooner because we were there—will something
else have grown?

Don't cry my doll don't cry
I hold you and rock you to sleep.
hush hush ~~I'm~~ I was only pretending now ~~that~~ I'm (was)
not your mother who died.

I shall feed you from the shiny dark bush
just left of the door.

After one year of analysis

Jamaica 36/78
Dr. Mike Fayer

Help Help
Help
I feel life coming closer
when all I want
is to die

scream—
You began and ended in acid
but where was the middle?

After one year of analysis

Help Help
Help
I feel life coming closer
when I all want
is to die.

Scream—
You began and ended in air
but where was the middle?

Notes:
It has been impossible to trace Dr. Mike Fayer.

According to Donald Spoto, Marilyn is thought to have sent the five-line poem "Help" to
Norman Rosten in the summer of 1961 after having started regular consultations with
Dr. Ralph Greenson. Spoto adds that Marilyn first wrote this poem, or perhaps message, in
Arthur Miller's notebook in London in 1956.

I'm not very bright I guess

No just dumb if I had
any brains I wouldn't be
on crummy train with this
crummy girls band

I used to sing with male
bands but I can't afford it
any more

Have you ever been with a
male band

Not

I'm not very bright I guess.

No just dumb//if I had
any brains I wouldn't be
on crummy train with this
crummy girls' band.

I used to sing with male
bands but I can't afford it
anymore.
Have you ever been with a male band

Heats

Note: This is a line from the scene in the train near
the beginning of *Some Like It Hot*.

you know I'm going to be
twenty five in June

You know I'm going to be
twenty-five in June

Note: This is also a line from *Some Like It Hot*. When the film was made Marilyn had turned
thirty-two, but her birthday was June 1.

Title - About my poems

Norman - so hard to please
When all I want is to tease
so it might rhyme
so What's the crime?
After all this
when I've spend all this time
on earth

Title—<u>About my poems</u>.

Norman—so hard to please
when all I want is to tease
<u>so</u> it might rhyme
so what's the crime?
~~When I've spent all this~~ After all this time
on earth

Note: Norman Rosten, poet and novelist, had been a close friend
of Marilyn's in New York since 1955.

Marilyn Monroe with Carson McCullers, during a lunch given by the American author in honor of
the great Danish writer Karen Blixen (Isak Dinesen), at McCullers's home in Nyack, New York, 1959
Marilyn with Blixen and McCullers

FRAGMENTS AND NOTES

The notes and fragments written here and there—
on torn-out pages, envelopes, tickets, address
books—bring together secrets, observations, efforts
at self-motivation and introspection. They also show
Marilyn's will, which was bent sometimes on purely
practical matters and at other times on the general
question of self-discipline. Ways of interpreting one
line or other, confusion at having to act a joyful part
when she felt sad, the need to concentrate harder,
birthday greetings with all kinds of fanciful names
(she loved inventing nicknames for her friends or
herself), memories of her mother wanting to keep
her out of the way, rules for life and work, reminders
for fittings for a gala evening dress, instructions for
her business partner Milton Greene, and, at the
beginning of an address book, a list of instructions
to be followed: in each text we glimpse a moment of
her life, a character trait, signs of doubt or
uneasiness, and, over and over, the desire to
improve and transform herself.

Aug 21

I am restless and nervous and scattered and jumpy.

A few minutes ago I almost threw a silver plate into a dark area on the set - but I knew couldn't afford to let out anything I really felt infact I wouldn't dare because I wouldn't stop at that maybe. Just before that I almost threw up my whole lunch. I'm tired. I'm searching for a way to play this part. I am depressed with my whole life since I first remember - How can I be such a gay young hopeful girl - What I am using is that

one sunday when I was fourteen for I was all those things that day but. Why can't I use it more consistantly my concentration wavers most of the time - something is racing in me in the opposite direction to most of the days I can remember. I must try to work and work on my concentration - maybe starting with the simplest of things.

Aug 27

I am restless and nervous and scattered and jumpy—a few minutes ago I almost threw a silver plate—into a dark area on the set—but I knew couldn't afford to let out anything I really felt in fact I wouldn't dare because I wouldn't stop at that maybe. Just before that I almost threw up my whole lunch. I'm tired. I'm searching for a way to play this part I am depressed with my whole life since I first remember— How can I be such a gay young hopeful girl—What I am using is that one sunday when I was fourteen for I was all these things that day but—Why can't I use it more consistently my concentration wavers most of the time—something is racing in me in the opposite direction to most of the days I can remember. I must try to work and work on my concentration—maybe starting with the simplest of things.

must have discipline. Must make effort to do
2- go to class — my own always — without fail.
x - go as often as possible to observe
Strassberg's other private classes.
3 - never miss actors studio sessions.
v - work whenever possible - or class assignments - and always keep working on the acting exer-
u - Start attending Clurman lectures —
also Lee Strassberg's directors lectures
of theater - come - I enquire about both.
l - Keep looking about me - only much more
sure observing - but not only myself but
others and everything - take things for what
they are worth
Y - must make strong effort to work on
current problems and phobias out of my past
has arisen - making much much more human -
more more more more effort in my
analiseis. And be there always on time -
no excuses for being ever late.
w - If possible - take at least one class at
University in literature —

Firenze · Milano

Via della Vigna Nuova, 47 · Via Monte Napoleone, 5
Follow R.C.A. thing through.

Roma · New York

Via Condotti, 21 · 7 East 58th Street at Fifth Avenue

R - try to find someone to take dancing
from - body work (practice) - personally -
Body Consciousness
T - Take care of my instrument -

Words - Find out their meanings 7/3/4
Wanderjahre - pertaining somehow to the
word Entsagung (what does
that mean to)? does it mean
Sacrifice.
à trois does it mean like - probation

Must make effort to do
must have the discipline to do the following—
z – go to class—my own <u>always</u>—without fail
x – go as often as possible to observe Strasberg's other private classes
g – <u>never</u> miss my actors studio sessions
v – <u>work</u> whenever possible—on class assignments—and <u>always keep working on the</u>
<u>acting exercises.</u>
u – start attending Clurman lectures—also Lee Strasberg's directors' lectures at theater
wing—enquire about both
l – keep looking around me—only much more so—<u>observing</u>—but not only myself but
others and everything—take things (it) for what they (it's) are worth.
y – must make strong effort to work on current problems and phobias that out of my
past has arisen—making much much much more more more more more effort in my
analysis. And be there <u>always</u> on time—no excuses for being <u>ever</u> late.
w – if possible take at least one class at university—in literature—
o – follow RCA thing through.
p – try to find someone to take dancing from—body work (creative)
t – take care of my instrument—personally & bodily (exercise)

try to enjoy myself when I can—I'll be miserable enough as it is.

Words—Find out their meanings

<u>Wanderjahre</u>—pertaining somehow to the
            word <u>Entsagung</u>—(what does
            that mean to)? does it mean
            sacrifice.

<u>à trois</u>   does it mean like—probation

Notes:
The names in this address book, especially that of Milton Greene, would seem to
indicate that it was bought in New York in 1955.

Harold Clurman, theater director and drama critic, was one of the three founders of
Group Theatre in New York in 1931 (along with Lee Strasberg).

Marilyn Monroe signed a contract to record film songs with the RCA label in 1954.

There is no obvious link between "Wanderjahre" (the wandering years) and
"Entsagung" (renunciation), unless Marilyn is echoing her reading of Freud or Rilke.

"À trois"/"threesome" bears at most a dubious connection with "probation."

12:00 Cecil Chapman –

530 7th Ave. –
4th floor

tel # LA-4-5800

Saturday Morning 12:00 –

Sunday Night Actors Benifit at least
dinner for them some where? ask
speak to Paula – about scenes
for me in the future

Monday Night

Hair – instead of the one done on Mon.
Dress – morning – also ask about
comb out for Mon Night

Saturday Afternoon 2:30
Lee Strasberg Matenee
Cat on hot tin Roof
Sat Morn – Profile time – call about then

Fri Night –
John Moore Fitting

Fri Morning
8:30 Francisco Hair
11:00 Actors Studio

Call Milton about –

1 – Clean a week with Kleinberg
– Saturday – because leaving and
need it and she willing

2 – About paying Hohenberg's
Bill – which didn't give him
yet (Could say it on Mon?)

3 – About white shoes because
probably wear white dress
(what about wrap?)

Call Lois, & Peter & Jacobs
about Yesterday papers
mainly Herald & News times.

12:00 Ceil Chapman—
530 7th ave—
4th floor
tel # LA–4–5800

Saturday Morning 12:00
Sunday Night—Actors Benefit
dinner for them somewhere? At least ask
speak to Paula—about scenes for me in
the future

Monday Night
Hair—instead of tues. have done
on Mon. morning—also ask about
comb out for Mon. night.
Dress—
Saturday afternoon 2:30
Lee Strasberg matinee
Cat on a Hot Tin Roof
Sat Morn—Profile time call about then
C. Chapman

Fri Night
John Moore fitting

Fri Morning
8:30—Francis [illegible] Hair
11:00 Actors Studio

Call Milton about—
1—6 days a week with Hohenberg—
Saturdays—because learning and need
it and she willing
2—about paying Hohenbergs—
Bill—which didn't give him
yet—(can we pay it on Mon?)
3—about white shoes because probably
wear white dress
(what about wrap?)

Call Lois Weber or A. Jacobs
about all yesterday's papers
mainly Herald Trib and Times

Notes:
This note was probably written in December 1955, as the Actors Studio benefit party was held in New York on December 12, to which, however, Marilyn wore a black dress (see photo on page 192).

Paula Strasberg, Lee Strasberg's wife, was also a very close friend and became Marilyn's coach during film shoots.

Ceil Chapman has often been said to have been Marilyn's favorite fashion designer.

John Moore, couturier and interior designer, decorated the Millers' apartment at 444 East 57th Street in 1955. He created several dresses for Marilyn, including the wedding dress she wore when she married Arthur Miller.

Arthur Jacobs, who was head of his own company, took care of public relations for Marilyn from 1955 until her death.

Lois Weber, who worked for the Arthur P. Jacobs Company, was Marilyn's press agent in New York.

For Iris   James 12th Birthday one 7th
Sept 9   some years

– Remember somehow how
Mother always tried to
get me to "go out" as
though she felt I
were too unadventurous.
She wanted me even
to show a cruelty
toward woman. This
in my terms. In return,
I showed her that I
was faithful to her.

For Kris
Sept. 9

Jane's 12th birthday on 7th
same year

—Remember, somehow, how—
Mother always tried to
get me to "go out" as
though she felt I
were too unadventurous.
She wanted me even
to show a cruelty
toward woman. This
in my teens. In return,
I showed her that I
was faithful to her.

Notes:
Kris was undoubtedly Dr. Marianne Kris, Marilyn's New York analyst from 1956 to February 1961.

Jane Miller, Arthur's elder daughter, was born on September 7, 1944; therefore, this note must have been written in 1956.

for life

It is rather a
determination not to
be overwhelmed.

for Work

The truth can only
be recalled, never
invented

<u>for life</u>
It is rather a determination not to be overwhelmed.

for <u>work</u>
The truth can only be recalled, never invented

forgive us for being
sentimental

if one

Hope this finds you feeling
just great - no-that- not what
I want to say - I mean - Forgive me
Youve got style - the way youve
moved along these years-
slow me up

Mate   for being sentimental
late
Rate-   I'm so glad you were born
ate   and that I'm living at the
             Same time as you-

~~Happy Birthday~~ Love (we all love you)
                        Noodle
                        Sam
                        Max
                        Clump
                        Scoyu finny
                        pussy
                        and all the rest
~~No I mean I mean~~   of us - -

Forgive us for being sentimental
if only

Hope this finds you feeling
just great—no that's not what
I want to say [~~illegible~~]—I mean—forgive me

for being sentimental
I'm so glad you were born
and that I'm ~~alive~~ living at the
same time as you.

You've got style—the way you've
moved along these years.
Slow me up
Mate
Late
Rate
ate

~~Happy Birthday~~ Love (we all love you)
Noodle
~~no I mean I mean~~ Sam
Max
Clump
Sugar Finny
Pussy
and all the rest
of us . . .

Note: This short prose piece and the variation on it on the following page were very likely written on the occasion of Norman Rosten's birthday. "She gave herself pretty names. One day, she signed a note with Noodle, Sam, Max, Clump, Sugar Finny, Pussy, and so on. An identity name, the little funny imp. It was a very attractive aspect of her personality: she had a great sense of humor" (Norman Rosten, *Marilyn Among Friends*).

its time for
            statement
I know how statements
we feel

                intrumental
                sentimental
        merely incidental
            coinmental
not a tear you'll see
forgive me if I'm

influence by tender feeling
affecting the (emotions)
            senamental.
mean — influences! tender
    feeling   Happy Birthday
                        (we all love you)
ourselves or myself   Sam
Sense   — Max
                    Clamp.
Sensable - sensitive   Sugar Penny

It's time for
sentiment
I know how sentimental we feel

                                   instrumental
                                   sentimental
                             merely incidental
                                   coincidental

Not a tear you'll see
Forgive me if I'm

influence by tender feelings
affecting the emotions
meaning—sentimental is a influenced for
tender
feelings
ourselves or myself

            sense
                              Happy birthday and love (we all love you)
sensible—sensitive   Noodle
                                                  Sam
                                                  Max
                                                Clump
                                            Sugar Finny
                                                 Pussy
                                    and all the rest of us—

darts dream –
2 ⊄ 2
2 ⊄ 3
Feb 28

Dec 11
    See in older journal – +
Always admired men who
had many women
    It must be that to a
child of a dissatisfied woman
the idea of monogamy
is hollow –

Starts dream—
262
263
Feb 28

Dec 11
See in older journal—
always admired men who had many women.
It must be that to a child of a dissatisfied woman
the idea of monogamy is hollow

Note: The numbers 262 and 263 probably refer to the same
collection of song standards as those on page 82 (the Waldorf-Astoria
series). The titles these correspond to are "While We're Young" (262)
and "Wonderful Guy" (263).

Pardon me – I'm sorry to wake you
But I wonder if you could help
me

I'm being Abducted

you know kidnapped – by him

I thought maybe as soon as
We got some place I'd ask the
driver to stop and let me off
But we been driving for hours
and we still don't seem to be
nowhere at all – Not only that
but I'm freezing to death – I
aint got much on under
my coat

Pardon me—I'm sorry to wake you
But I wonder if you could help
me

I'm being abducted

you know—kidnapped—by <u>him</u>

I thought maybe as soon as
we <u>got</u> some place I'd ask the
driver to stop and let me off
But we been driving for hours
and we still don't seem to be
nowhere at all—not only that
but I'm freezing to death—I
ain't got much on under
my coat

sleeping prince - for paula   learn-lines logically

don't stop Myself   – I can't do more Than
                       one thing at a time

Name tasks – 1 2 3 4 etc   make map tonight

T - weariness

                                    take my time
                                      to Think –

Write out part-copying it

Work on exercises
1-cold

Sleeping prince—for Paula

don't stop myself
Name tasks—1 - 2 - 3 - 4 etc.

T—weariness

write out part—copying it

work on exercises
1—cold

learn—lines **logically**

—I can't do more than
one thing at a time
make map tonight

take my time to think—

Note: *The Sleeping Prince* was the first title for *The Prince and the Showgirl*, which was filmed in London in 1956. This note must have been written the same year.

He said that so
became Identical
that as a sex symbol
public. never except me as
a virgin and as a footstool nineteen year old
+ mummy

he wants to
feel he discovers
and healone is
responsible
reality
is better

Eli
9— his lose
tennesse — wants me

tells Eli
new ending

I don't what anybody else

He said that
I've become so deified
as a sex symbol
that public never **accept** me as
a virgin and as a nineteen/twenty year old

                he wants to
                feel he discovers   reality
                and he alone is   is better
                responsible

Eli
g—his lose
tennesse**e**—wants me

tells Eli—
        new ending

I don't want anybody else

Note: Marilyn wanted to play the title role in Elia Kazan's 1956 film *Baby Doll*, written by
Tennessee Williams and starring Eli Wallach. However, Carroll Baker got the part.

I feel the camera has got
to look through Gay's
eyes Whenever he is in a
scene and even when he is
not - there still have to get a sense of
him

He is the center and the
rest move around him

but I guess Houston will
see to that

he is both subtle and
overt in his leading them
and his cruelty and his tenderness
(when he reaches out of himself
for her - R.)

I feel the camera has got
to look through Gay's
eyes whenever he is in a
scene and even when he is
not there still has to be a sense of
him
He is the center and the
rest move around him
but I guess Houston will
see to that
He is both subtle and
overt in his leading them
and in his cruelty and his tenderness
(when he reaches out of himself
for her—R.)

Notes:
John Huston's (here spelled "Houston") film *The Misfits* was shot in Nevada, in the summer of 1960. Arthur Miller adapted the script from his own short story, the role of Roslyn having been inspired by his wife. The atmosphere was extremely tense, especially between the couple, whose marriage was foundering. Marilyn, a perfectionist, was frequently late—very late—frightened of not being ready for the challenge, and often groggy from the barbiturates she had begun to depend on. She was awestruck to be acting with Clark Gable, who was a lifelong idol and whom she had sometimes thought of, or dreamed of, as her own father. Marilyn had already been directed by John Huston in *The Asphalt Jungle*, the film that, in spite of a minor role, had put her name in lights. In a sense, in *The Misfits* she acted out her own life with a disquieting and magnificent closeness that must have been enormously tormenting.

It is likely that this note was written during the first half of the shooting, in July. Gay (Langland) is the name of the character played by Clark Gable. The final "R" refers to Roslyn (Taber), Marilyn's character.

KITCHEN NOTES

1955 or 1956

Contrary to the image we may have of Marilyn as often disorderly and chaotic, she attended to some aspects of daily life with care and even meticulousness. When she had to decorate an apartment or house she made notes, took measurements, collected samples or patterns, and decided on color schemes and the arrangement of furniture. Similarly, when she organized a dinner for Helen Schneider's birthday, very likely at the end of 1955 in New York, she wrote a long, exacting list of everything she had to prepare or check out. Each detail was planned, down to the table decorations and bathroom requisites. This party may have taken place when Marilyn moved into an apartment on the corner of Sutton Place and 57th Street after her long stay in a suite at the Waldorf-Astoria, which had turned out to be too costly for Marilyn Monroe Productions. Incidentally, Marilyn sometimes enjoyed cooking, and when she did she noted recipes down to the last ingredient, step by step, including the quality of produce needed.

ask for Kitty for Clyde (?) (from last
My white dishes - all of them part
My old silver candle holders
My paintings two - b got an drunken dutch women Angels
Get fire wood - What about silverware -
buy - White toilet seat
buy - hamper or good thing for bathroom & thing for & back of dirt towels, toilley etc.
buy - lamps for bedroom & the shades take Kirt with me -
buy foot stool & coffee table (ask Mamouimu yon)
buy bed buy mirrored at Le tay lke
buy two chairs - classic - for in front of piano. also serves for extra guest chairs
buy brass ash trays one for M-one Clarke - one for me
buy Chandliers - one for hall - one for dinning area take back the two glasses silver things
buy twelve linnin napkins - Silverware for 12
buy Birthday present for Helen -

have Kirt paint places for Chandlieres also where broke railing
have Milton & Kirt put pictures in hallway - help
me arrange room - & place
have - Kirt saw off legs of Candle Holders

dry clean -
    comforter
have Wash -
    bathroom rugs
send out laundry

ask for Kitty & or Clyde
my white dishes—all of them from Westport
my old silver candle holders
my <u>paintings</u> two—dutch woman big one and drunken angels
get firewood—what about silverware
buy—white toilet seat
buy—hamper & or gold thing for bathroom & or thing for back of door
                                                    for towels, bottles, etc

buy—lamps for bedroom—also shades take Kirt with me
buy foot stool & coffee table (ask M. Moumulion)
buy bar buy mirror at L. & Taylors
buy two chairs—classic—for in front of piano, also serves for extra guest chairs
buy brass ash trays one for M. one for L. one for me
buy chandeliers—one for hall—one for dining area—take back the two glass silver
things
buy twelve linen napkins—silverware—for 12
buy birthday present for Helen—

have Kirt paint places for chandeliers also where railing broke
have Milton & Kirt put pictures in hallway—help me arrange room & place
have Kirt saw off legs of brass candle holders

dry clean comforter
have wash—bathroom rugs
send out laundry

call Moumulion
<u>guest towels</u>
paintings 2

coffee table
[indecipherable] glass bar

Notes:
Kitty and Clyde may have provided Marilyn with occasional help.

Kirt seems to have been a man who did odd jobs for Marilyn.

M. Moumulion: unidentified.

The reference to Milton Greene would mean this birthday dinner took place between 1955
and 1956. Marilyn stayed at Milton and Amy Greene's property in Westport, Connecticut,
when she first arrived on the East Coast and often visited them in subsequent months.

Buy — liquor - Scotch - Gin - Vermouth | champane? | at least some kind of wine
with dinner

Ordoves - Caviar - others?

— two roasts - 1- prime ribs of beef 1- turkey
Have Hedda make dressing   with endive hearts
large mixed green salad - avacado? (Also aspic?
— not done too well
Vetables - Frozen peas or in pol? — kittys squash? or something
Potatoes - of some kind - ? ask kitty
Celery hearts - olives — scallions? - Radishes
ask Hedda about
Fruit & Ice cream for dessert - choc. & vinella
Coffee & cookies & danish pastry for later
Birthday Cake for Helen -
Geo. Leslie   & me   2
Hedda & Norman   2
E Hores Sessie   2
Helen + Isadore   2
George Brasilla + wife   2
Guy + friend with guitar 2

(Murry hill - 25 4 00
French prov. white
Marble top 25 12 03
coffee table
Buy for less
than he says.

Blomindales
wine glasses 12
Tin ne Whiskeys   Ivory. Flakes or snow
for more
lowest fausets   Rins 6 Blue or detergent

champagne? at least some kind of wine with dinner
buy—liquor—scotch—gin—vermouth—
hors d'œuvres—caviar—others?

two roasts— 1—prime ribs of beef 1—turkey
have Hedda make dressing
large mixed green salad with endive hearts—avocado? (Also aspic?)
vegetables—frozen peas or in pod?—not done too well—Kitty's squash? or something
Potatoes—of some kind—? ask Kitty
Celery hearts—olives—scallions?—Radishes
ask Hedda about fruit & ice cream for dessert—choc & vanilla
Coffee & cookies & danish pastry for later
Birthday cake for Helen—
Geo. Leslie & me   2
Hedda & Norman 2   Murray Hill—25400
Ettore & Jessie 2   french prov. white
Helen & Isadore 2   marble top 2 sizes
George Brusilla **[Braziller]** & wife 2   coffee table
Guy & friend with guitar 2   buy for less than he says
                                                       Lloyds 116 E 60th

Bloomingdales?
Wine glasses 12
linen napkins   Ivory. Flakes or snow
6 or more guest towels   Rinso Blue or detergent

Notes:
Geo. Leslie: unidentified.

Isadore Schneider (1896–1976) was born in the Ukraine and emigrated with his family to the
United States in 1904. A novelist and critic, he was a friend of Norman Rosten's, knew Arthur
Miller, and worked as a reader for George Braziller at Grove Press. Helene Berlin Schneider
was his wife.

Ettore Rella (1907–1988) was a poet and playwright. His wife was named Jessie.

George Braziller was born in 1916 and founded his own publishing house in 1955. His wife
was Marsha.

Guy: unidentified.

CITY TITLE INSURANCE COMPANY

68 SUTTER STREET ——— Phone GArfield 1-8530

"Complete Title and Escrow Service"

No garlic

sour dough

for French Bread - soak in cold water

chicken then shed,

giblets - boil in water - 5-10 min

liver

heart

then chop

1 whole or 1/2 onion - chop & parsarly

four stalk celery chop together

following spices - put in the more

thyme - bay leaf - oregano - poultry season

(parmisiach)

salt - pepper - Gratted cheese - 1 handful

1/2 lb - 1/4 lb Ground round - put in frying

pan - brown (no oil) then mix

rasian 1 1/2 cups or more

walnuts

chestnuts { 1 cup chop nuts

pinuts

1 or 2 hard boiled eggs - chopped

mix together salt & pepper inside chicken

or turkey - outside same & butter

no garlic
sourdough
french bread—soak in cold water wring out
then shred

for chicken giblets—boil in water—5–10 min.
liver heart then chop

1 whole or ½ onion—chop & parsley four stalk celery chop together
following spices—put in rosemary
thyme—bay leaf—oregano—poultry seasoning—salt—pepper—
grated Parmesan cheese—1 handful
½ lb.—¼ lb ground round—put in frying pan—brown (no oil) then mix
raisin 1½ cups or more
walnuts
chestnuts ⎱1 cup chop nuts
peanuts

1 or 2 hard boiled eggs—chopped
mix together

salt & pepper inside chicken

or turkey—outside same and butter

>>>

Sew up or clamp birds

put chicken or turkey in 350° oven

Roasting
chicken - 3 or 4 lbs. or larger
cooks 30 min to 1 lbs

Vinegar

oil   ⎫ brown chicken
onion ⎬   or phesant
spices ⎭

let cook in own juice

add little water as you go

½ glass vinigar - put in when half
                        don

cooks 2 hours.

put potatoes

mushroom - button canned

peas - fresh

>>>

sew up or clamp birds
put chicken or turkey in 350° oven
roasting chicken—3 or 4 lbs. or larger
cooks   30 min to 1 lbs.

Vinegar
oil   { brown chicken
onion   or pheasant
spices

let cook in own juice
add little water as you go
½ glass vinegar—put in when half done
cooks 2 hours
put potatoes
mushroom—button canned
peas—fresh

LEE AND PAULA STRASBERG

When Marilyn arrived in New York at the beginning of 1955, she soon found her heart's dream: the Actors Studio, which she hoped would open the doors to a new status as an artist. Just as quickly, Lee Strasberg saw how exceptional she was, bursting with a talent seeking to express itself fully. However, Marilyn had a major shortcoming: she was always late. Lee had his reservations about this, and when she admitted that she was absolutely unable to be on time, he replied cuttingly: "Well, be early then." This explains the playful tone of the brief text in which she quotes a line from one of her early films that speaks of punctuation instead of punctuality . . .

The fragile confidence she developed often shifted to anguish and despair. What would happen if she lost her concentration, the only thing that kept an actor from suicide, to repeat Lee Strasberg's striking phrase? In February 1961, Marilyn thought she was checking into the hospital for a rest cure but instead found herself confined to a psychiatric cell at Payne Whitney in New York. Her friends couldn't respond to her cry for help, as, legally speaking, they weren't family members (Joe DiMaggio, whom she had divorced in 1954, would finally rescue her from this nightmare). In any case, Marilyn proved single-minded. Prompted by her sense of having escaped from quicksand, in a resolute letter to Lee Strasberg dated December 19, 1961, she laid out her plan for a new independent production company, which would make sense to her only if Lee were associated with it. To the very end, she wanted to be free of the studios, but this time she wanted to challenge them on their turf, in Hollywood.

Yes. Mr Oxly is always
complaining about my punctuation
so I'm careful to get here
before 9'00 — Mr. Oxly is on
telephone won't you sit down

loose letting go
voice starts back there

Don't be nervous Marilyn
you are doing swell &
you look wonderful —
                    L.

Oh yes Mr. Oxley is <u>always</u>
complaining about my <u>punctuation</u>
so ~~now~~ <u>I'm careful to get here</u>
before <u>9:00</u>. Mr. Oxley is on
telephone won't you sit down

loose letting go
voice starts back theatre

[following is written by Lee Strasberg]
Don't be nervous Marilyn
you are doing swell &
you look wonderful—
        L.

Notes:
The chronically late pupil used this line from *Monkey Business* (the 1952 Howard Hawks film in which Mr. Oxley is Marilyn's director) with no little humor when addressing her teacher (who may have been speaking on the telephone at that moment).

To judge by his reply, it is not clear that Lee Strasberg understood either the allusion or the quotation.

Dear Lee

~~#~~ One of the most personally helpful
things I've heard so far in my
life was what you said in
class friday afternoon - It was helpful in
~~that I feel as though Im a little~~
~~bit freeer - er more - I can't~~
~~Think ~~ ~~~~ ~~say I mean by that~~
More ~~relaxed~~ 2 and 2 dont
necessarily make 4.

Dear Lee

One of the most personally helpful things I've heard so far in my life was what you said in class friday afternoon—it was helpful ~~in that I feel as though I'm a little bit freer—also more—I can't think of any I mean by that more relaxed~~ 2 and 2 don't necessarly make 4.

Paula dear,

You asked me yesterday why —

I felt somehow (I'm only conscious of it this morning) that if I didn't have the control or the will to make myself do anything & do it right — I would never be able to act or do anything — I know it sounds crazy — maybe it was even superstitious I don't know — I don't know anything

Something has happened I think to make me lose my confidence. I don't know what it is.

All I know is I want to work

Oh paula I wish I knew why I am so anguished. I think maybe I am crazy like all the other members of my family were, when I was sick I was sure I was.

I am so glad you are with me here!

Paula dear,

You asked me yesterday why—

I felt somehow (I'm only conceiving of it this morning) that if I didn't have the control or the will to make myself do anything simple & do it right I would never be able to act or do anything—I know it sounds crazy—maybe it was even superstitious—I don't know—I don't know anything.

Something has happened I think to make me lose my confidence. I don't know what it is. All I know is I want to work.

Oh Paula I wish I knew why I am so anguished. I think maybe I'm crazy like all the other members of my family were, when I was sick I was sure I was. I'm so glad you are with me here!

Marilyn Monroe with Paula and Lee Strasberg, New York, 1955

Hotel Bel-Air

  701 Stone Canyon Road, Los Angeles 24

Dear Lee,

      I'm embarrised to start this, but thank you
for understanding and having changed my life -
even though you changed it I still am lost -
I mean I can't get myself together - I think
its because everything is pulling against my
concentration - everything one does or lives is
impossible almost.
      You once said, the first time I heard you
talk at the actors studio that "there is only
concentration between the actor and suiside."
As soon as I walk into a scene I lose my mental
relaxation for some reason, - which is my
concentration. My will is weak but I can't
stand anything. I sound crazy but I think
I'm going crazy.
      Thanks for letting Paula help me on the
picture she is the only really warm woman I've
known. Its just that I get before camera and
my concentration and everything I'm trying to
learn leaves me. Then I feel like I'm not
existing in the human race at all.

                  Love,

                  Marilyn

Note: It is very likely that this letter was written at the beginning of 1956, during the filming
of Joseph Logan's *Bus Stop*, when Paula Strasberg worked as Marilyn's coach for the
first time.

Dear Lee & Paula,

Dr Kris has had me put into the New York Hospital - particiatric divisian under the care of two idiot doctors. they both should not be my doctors.

You haven't heard from me because I'm locked up with all these poor nutty people. I'm sure to end up a nut if I stay in this nightmare - please help me Lee, this is the last place I should be - maybe if you called Dr Kris and accused her of my senility and that I must get back to class so I'll be better prepared for ruin

over

Lee, I try to remember what you said once in class "that art goes far beyond science"

And the scene memories around here I'd like to forget - like annoying woman &c.

please help me - if Dr Kris assures you I am all right - you can assure her I am not I do not belong here!

I love you both,

Marf

P.S. forgive the spelling - and there's nothin to write on here I'm on the disgrace floor !!! its like a cell can you imagine - cement block they put me in here because they lied to me about calling my Anita & Joe and they had the bathroom door locked so I broke the glass to get out of here & havn't done anything that warrens imprisonment

Dear Lee & Paula,

Dr. Kris has had me put into the New York Hospital—psychiatric division under the care of two <u>idiot</u> doctors—they <u>both should not be my doctors</u>.

You haven't heard from me because I'm locked up with all these poor nutty people. I'm sure to end up a nut if I stay in this nightmare—please help me Lee, this is the <u>last</u> place I should be—maybe if you called Dr. Kris and assured her of my sensitivity and that I must get back to class so I'll be better prepared for "Rain."

Lee, I try to remember what you said once in class "that art goes far beyond science."

And the scary memories around me I'd like to forget—like screaming woman etc.

Please help me—if Dr. Kris assures you I am all right—you can assure her <u>I am not</u>. I do not belong here!

        I love you both.

        Marilyn

P.S. forgive the spelling—and there is nothing to write on here. I'm on the dangerous floor!! It's like a cell can you imagine—cement blocks. They put me in here because they lied to me about calling my doctor & Joe and they had the bathroom door locked so I broke the glass and outside of that I haven't done anything that is uncooperative

Note: *Rain*, adapted from a Somerset Maugham short story, was a TV project that Lee Strasberg hoped to direct. Marilyn Monroe and John Gielgud were to have had the main parts. The film was never made because of a disagreement between NBC and Lee Strasberg.

December 19, 1961

Mr. Lee Strasberg
135 Central Park West
New York 23, New York

Dear Lee:

This is an important personal letter and please don't
start to read it until you have the time to give it your careful thought. This letter concerns my future plans and
therefore concerns yours as well since my future development
as an artist is based on our working together. All this is
an introduction; let me outline the recent events, my ideas
and my suggestions.

As you know, for years I have been struggling to find
some emotional security with little success, for many different
reasons. Only in the last several months, as you detected, do
I seem to have made a modest beginning. It is true that my
treatment with Dr. Greenson has had its ups and downs, as you
know. However, my overall progress is such that I have hopes
of finally establishing a piece of ground for myself to stand
on, instead of the quicksand I have always been in. But
Dr. Greenson agrees with you, that for me to live decently
and productively, I must work! And work means not merely
performing professionally, but to study and truly devote myself.
My work is the only trustworthy hope I have. And here, Lee,
is where you come in. To me, work and Lee Strasberg are
synonymous. I do not want to be presumptuous in expecting
you to come out here for me alone. I have contacted Marlon
on this subject and he seems to be quite interested, despite
the fact that he is in the process of finishing a movie. I
shall talk with him more thoroughly in a day or two.

Furthermore, and this must be kept confidential for
the time being, my attorneys and I are planning to set up and
independent production unit, in which we have envisaged an
important position for you. This is still in the formative
phase, but I am thinking of you in some consultative position
or in whatever way you might see fit. I know you will want
enough freedom to pursue your teaching and any other private
interests you might want to follow.

Though I am committed to my analysis, as painful as
it is, I cannot definitively decide, until I hear from you,
because without working with you only half of me is functioning.
Therefore, I must know under what conditions you might consider
coming out here and even settling here.

2

I know this might sound quite fantastic, but if you add up all the possible advantages it should be a quite rewarding venture. I mean not only for Marlon and me -- but for others. This independent production unit will also be making pictures without me -- this is even required for legal reasons. This will offer an opportunity for Susan if she should be interested and perhaps even for Johnny. And Paula would have a great many opportunities for coaching. As for you, Lee, I still have the dream of you some day directing me in a film! I know this is a big step to take, but I have the wish that you might realize out here some of the incomplete hopes that were perhaps not fulfilled for you, like Lincoln Center, etc.

So I don't know how else to persuade you. I need you to study with and I am not alone in this. I want to do everything in my power to get you to come out -- within reason -- as long as it is to your advantage as well as mine. So, Lee, please think this over carefully; this is an awfully important time of my life and since you mentioned on the phone that you too felt things were unsettled, I have dared to hope.

I have meetings set up with Marlon and also with my attorneys and will phone you if there are any important new developments. Otherwise, please get in touch with me.

My love to all of you,

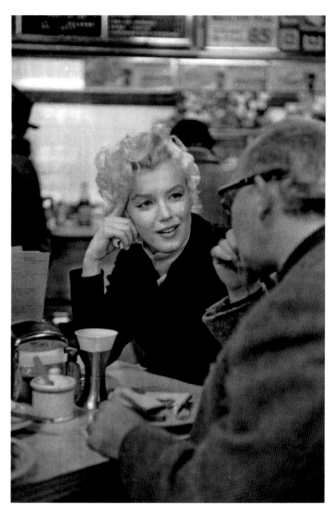

Marilyn Monroe and Lee Strasberg in a café
near Carnegie Hall in New York

LETTER TO DR. HOHENBERG

1956

Before accepting Marilyn as a student of his "Method,"
Lee Strasberg made it a condition that she start
psychoanalysis. From the spring of 1955, therefore, three
to five times a week, the actress consulted Dr. Margaret
Hohenberg at 155 East 93rd Street in New York.
Margaret Hohenberg was born in 1898 in Slovakia and
had studied in Vienna, Budapest, and Prague before
having to flee Austria in 1938 after the Anschluss.
She first went to London for a year, then settled in
New York in 1939.

Milton Greene, one of Dr. Hohenberg's patients,
recommended her to Marilyn, and, curiously, the doctor
accepted her as an analysand in spite of the obvious risk
involved in treating two patients who not only knew each
other but also had very close professional links. In fact,
shortly after Milton Greene was fired from Marilyn Monroe
Productions, the actress stopped seeing the analyst and
never returned to her consulting rooms.

Nevertheless, a bill for $840, drawn up by
Dr. Hohenberg on August 1, 1962, indicates that Marilyn
had gotten back in touch with her former analyst for
telephone consultations.

Dear Dr Hohenberg

I've been wondering myself why I don't write to you ~ ~~Though it has to~~ ~~the fact that~~ ~~I've been~~ I was taken away from you (and ~~around~~) or that you sent me away from you —

On the whole, things are going along rather well <u>so far</u>

M.C.A., our agents, and ~~then, our lawyer~~ ~~are~~ now dealing with ~~stations~~ but — we'll see —

I have a strange feeling about paula I mean — she works differently than Lee Any way ~~and~~ I keep feeling I won't be

but she is a wonderful and warm person — which also ~~bewilderes me~~ able to do the part when I have too it like a horrible nightmare

Also I guess I didn't write you before this because I was waiting to see if I would get shot — first.

Arthur writes me every day — at least ~~that~~ it gives me ~~the air~~ air to breathe — I can't get use to the fact that he loves me and I keep waiting for him to stop ~~(long ago)~~ though I hope he never will — but I keep telling myself — who knows?

Dear Dr. Hohenberg,

I've been wondering myself why I don't write to you. ~~I think it has to do with the fact that~~ I've been feeling I was taken away from you (with your consent) or that you sent me away from you—

On the whole, things are going along rather well <u>so far</u>

M.C.A., our agents, and Stein, our lawyer ~~are dealing~~ have dealt with Natasha but—we'll see—

I have a strange feeling about Paula. I mean—she works differently than Lee but she is a wonderful and warm person—which also bewilders me

Anyway I keep feeling I won't be able to do the part when I have to it's like a horrible nightmare.

Also I guess I didn't write you before this because I was waiting to see if I would get shot first.

Arthur writes me every day—at least it gives me ~~a little~~ air to breathe—I can't get used to the fact that he loves me and I keep waiting for him to stop loving me—though I <u>hope</u> he never will—but I keep telling myself—who knows?

Notes:
In January 1953, Marilyn left the William Morris Agency, whose vice president, Johnny Hyde, had died in 1950. She signed a contract with the powerful talent agency MCA, Inc. (Music Corporation of America). George Chasin attended to Marilyn's interests at MCA until her death. In her book *Marilyn and Me*, Susan Strasberg quotes a story dating back to 1962 as told by Marilyn's masseur, Ralph Roberts: "She asked me if I had heard any rumors about Bobby Kennedy and herself. None of it is true, she told me. Besides, he is too skinny. Bobby is trying to dismantle MCA and has asked me to help him." Indeed, MCA had to wind down its agency work and concentrate on production after an action brought against the corporation by Attorney General Robert Kennedy in July 1962.

Irving Stein, along with Frank Delaney, was one of the lawyers who worked for Marilyn Monroe Productions.

In 1948, Natasha Lytess was appointed by Columbia, as was their usual practice, to help Marilyn prepare for her part in the Phil Karlson film *Ladies of the Chorus*. The two women worked together on about twenty films until Marilyn chose Paula Strasberg to assist her during the shooting of *Bus Stop* in February 1956. Natasha Lytess found it difficult to accept this break.

LETTER TO DR. GREENSON

1961

From January 1960 onward, following the advice of
Marianne Kris (her analyst in New York at that time),
Marilyn started analysis with Dr. Ralph Greenson in
Los Angeles. She wrote him a long letter on
March 2 and 3, 1961, about three weeks after
her disastrous confinement at Payne Whitney, when
she had had to confront one of her worst fears: the
specter of hereditary family madness, the fear of
ending up in a psychiatric hospital like her mother and
grandmother before her.
At the time, Marilyn had been transferred from Payne
Whitney after Joe DiMaggio's intercession and was
convalescing at Columbia University's Presbyterian
Medical Center. She was reading Freud, especially his
letters. Bed-bound, she wrote describing the details of
her confinement and all the misunderstandings that
had led to her being placed in isolation. We can
imagine her distress as she faced the guardians of
normalcy whom she felt were ready to condemn
her irrevocably. We are almost surprised at the
moderate tone she used when discussing Dr. Kris's
involvement, and the sense of perspective she had
when recalling a scene in *Don't Bother to Knock*
(directed by Roy Baker in 1952) that inspired her
rebellion against the commitment and her (sham)
suicide threat. We can find, too, in this poignant letter,
the characteristic way Marilyn would suddenly change
the subject to something positive in order to put her
fears to one side: here her reconciliation with
Joe DiMaggio, which had happened at Christmas.

Dear Dr. Greenson,

I'm having May Reis type this because

it's not very clearly written, but I have also

included these notes and you will see what I mean.

M.M.

March 2, 1961

Note: May Reis was Marilyn's personal assistant from the mid-1950s onward.

March 1,1961

    Just now when I looked out the hospital window where the snow
had covered everything suddenly everything is kind of a muted green.
The grass, shabby evergreen bushes -- though the trees give me a little
hope -- the desolate bare branches promising maybe there will be spring
and maybe they promise hope.

    Did you see "The Misfits" yet? In one sequence you can perhaps
see how bare and strange a tree can be for me. I don't know if it
comes across that way for sure on the screen -- I don't like some of
the selections in the takes they used. As I started to write this
letter about four quiet tears had fallen. I don't know quite why.

    Last night I was awake all night again. Sometimes I wonder what
the night time is for. It almost doesn't exist for me -- it all seems
like one long, long horrible day. Anyway, I thought I'd try to be
constructive about it and started to read the letters of Sigmund Freud.
When I first opened the book I saw the picture of Freud inside opposite
the title page and I burst into tears -- he looked very depressed (which
must have been taken near the end of his life) that he died a disappointed
man -- but Dr. Kris said he had much physical pain which I had known
from the Jones book -- but I know this too to be so but still I trust
my instincts because I see a sad disappointment in his gentle face.
The book reveals (though I am not sure anyone's love-letters should be
published) that he wasn't a stiff! I mean his gentle, sad humor and
even a striving was eternal in him. I haven't gotten very far yet because
at the same time I'm reading Sean O'Casey's first autobiography --(did
I ever tell you how once he wrote a poem to me?) This book disturbs me
very much in a way one should be disturbed for these things --after all,

    There was no empathy at Payne-Whitney -- it had a very bad effect
-- they asked me after putting me in a "cell" (I mean cement blocks and
all) for <u>very disturbed</u> depressed patients(except I/was in some kind
felt I

of prison for a crime I hadn't comitted. The inhumanity there I
found archaic. They asked me why I wasn't happy there (everything
was under lock and key; things like electric lights, dresser draws,
bathrooms, closets, bars concealed on the windows -- the doors have
windows so patients can be visible all the time, also, the violence
and markings still remain on the walls from former patients).
I answered: "Well, I'd have to be nuts if I like it here" then there
screaming women in their cells -- I mean they screamed out when life
was unbearable I guess -- at times like this I felt an available
psychiatrist should have talked to them. Perhaps to alleviate even
temporarily their misery and pain. I think they (the doctors) might
learn something even -- but all are only interested in something
from the books they studied -- I was surprised because they already
knew that! Maybe from some live suffering human being maybe they
could discover more -- I had the feeling they looked more for discipline
and that they let their patients go after the patients have "given
up". They asked me to mingle with the patients, to go out to O.T.
(Occupational Therapy). I said: "And do what?" They said: "You could
sew or play checkers, even cards and maybe knit". I tried to explain
the day I did that they would have a nut on their hands. These things
were furthest from my mind. They asked me why I felt I was "different"
(from the other patients, I guess) so I decided if they were really
that stupid I must give them a very simple answer so I said: "I just
am".

The first day I did "mingle" with a patient. She asked me why
I looked so sad and suggested I could call a friend and perhaps not
be so lonely. I told her that they had told me that there wasn't
a phone on that floor. Speaking of floors, they are all locked --
no one could go in and no one could go out. She looked shocked and
shaken and said "I'll take you to the phone" -- while I waited in line

for my turn for the use of the phone I observed a guard (since he had
on a gray knit uniform) as I approached the phone he straight-armed the
phone and said very sternly: "You can't use the phone". By the way,
they pride themselves in having a home-like atmosphere. I asked them
(the doctors) how they figured that. They answered: "Well, on the sixth
floor we have wall-to-wall carpeting and modern furniture" to which I
replied: "Well, that any good interior decorator could provide --
providing there are the funds for it" but since they are dealing with
human beings why couldn't they perceive even an interior of a human
being".

The girl that told me about the phone seemed such a pathetic and
vague creature. She told me after the straight-arming "I didn't know
they would do that". Then she said "I'm here because of my mental
condition -- I have cut my throat several times and slashed my wrists"
--she said either three or four times.

I just thought of a jingle:

"Mingle - but not if you
were just born single"

Oh, well, men are climbing to the moon but they don't seem interested
in the beating human heart. Still one can change but won't -- by the
way, that was the original theme of THE MISFITS -- no one even caught
that part of it. Partly because, I guess, the changes in the script
and some of the distortions in the direction and .....

LATER WRITTEN

I know I will never be happy but I know I can be gay! Remember
I told you Kazan said I was the gayest girl he ever knew and believe
me he has known many. But he loved me for one year and once rocked me
to sleep one night when I was in great anguish. He also suggested that
I go into analysis and later wanted me to work with his teacher, Lee
Strasberg.

Was it Milton who wrote: "The happy ones were never born"? I know

at least two psychiatrists who are looking for a more positive
approach.

THIS MORNING, MARCH 2

I didn't sleep again last night. I forgot to tell you something
yesterday. When they put me into the first room on the sixth floor
I was not told it was a Psychiatric floor. Dr. Kris said she was coming
the next day. The nurse came in (after the doctor, a psychiatrist)
had given me a physical examination including examining the breast for
lumps. I took exception to this but not violently only explaining that
the medical doctor who had put me there, a stupid man named Dr. Lipkin
had already done a complete physical less than thirty days before.
But when the nurse came in I noticed there was no way of buzzing or
reaching for a light to call the nurse. I asked why this was and some
other things and she said this is a psychiatric floor. After she went
out I got dressed and then was when the girl in the hall told me about
the phone. I was waiting at the elevator door which looks like all
other doors with a door-knob except it doesn't have any numbers (you
see they left them out). After the girl spoke with me and told me
about what she had done to herself I went back into my room knowing they
had lied to me about the telephone and I sat on the bed trying to figure
if I was given this situation in an acting improvisation what would I
do. So I figured, it's a squeaky wheel that gets the grease. I admit
it was a loud squeak but I got the idea from a movie I made once called
"Don't Bother to Knock". I picked up a light-weight chair and slammed
it, and it was hard to do because I had never broken anything in my
life -- against the glass intentionally. It took a lot of banging to
get even a small piece of glass - so I went over with the glass concealed in my hand and sat quietly on the bed waiting for them to come
in. They did, and I said to them "if you are going to treat me like a

nut I'll act like a nut". I admit the next thing is corny but I
really did it in the movie except it was with a razor blade. I indicated
if they didn't let me out I would harm myself -- the furthest thing
from my mind at that moment since you know Dr. Greenson I'm an actress
and would never intentionally mark or mar myself, I'm just that vain.
Remember when I tried to do away with myself I did it very carefully
with ten seconal and ten tuonal and swallowed them with relief (that's
how I felt at the time.) I didn't cooperate with them in any way
because I couldn't believe in what they were doing. They asked me to
go quietly and I refused to move staying on the bed so they picked me
up by all fours, two hefty men and two hefty women and carried me up
to the seventh floor in the elevator. I must say at least they had the
decency to carry me face down. You know at least it wasn't face up.
I just wept quietly all the way there and then was put in the cell I
told you about and that ox of a woman one of those hefty ones said:
"Take a bath". I told her I had just taken one one the sixth floor.
She said very sternly: "As soon as you change floors you have to take
another bath". The man who runs that place, a high-school principal
type, although Dr. Kris refers to him as an "administrator" he was
actually permitted to talk to me, questioning me somewhat like an analyst.
He told me I was a very, very sick girl and had been a very, very sick
girl for many years. He looks down on his patients because I'll tell you
why in a moment. He asked me how I could possibly work when I was
depressed. He wondered if that interfered with my work. He was being
very firm and definite in the way he said it. He actually stated it
more than he questioned me so I replied: "Didn't he think that perhaps
Greta Garbo and Charlie Chaplin perhaps and perhaps Ingrid Bergman they
had been depressed when they worked sometimes but I said it's like saying
a ball player like DiMaggio if he could hit ball when he was depressed.
Pretty silly.

6

By the way, I have some good news, sort of, since I guess I helped, he claims I did. Joe said I saved his life by sending him to a psycho-therapist; Dr. Kris says he is a very brilliant man, the doctor. Joe said he pulled himself up by his own bootstraps after the divorce but he told me also that if he had been me he would have divorced him too. Christmas night he sent a forest-full of poinsettias. I asked who they were from since it was such a surprise,(my friend Pat Newcomb was there)-- they had just arrived then. She said: "I don't know the card just says "best, Joe". Then I replied: "Well, there's just one Joe". Because it was Christmas night I called him up and asked him why he had sent me the flowers. He said first of all because I thought you would call me to thank me and then he said, besides who in the hell else do you have in the world. He said I know I was married to you and was never bothered or saw any in-law. Anyway, he asked me to have a drink some time with him. I said I knew he didn't drink -- he said he now ocasionally takes a drink -- to which I replied then it would have to be a very, very dark place. He asked me what I was doing Christmas night. I said nothing, I'm here with a friend. Then he asked me to come over and I was glad he was coming though I must say I was bleary and depressed but somehow still glad he was coming over.

I think I had better stop because you have other things to do but thanks for listening for a while.

Marilyn M.

PS: Someone when I mentioned his name you used to frown with your moustache and look up at the ceiling. Guess who? He has been (secretly) a very tender friend. I know you won't believe this but you must trust me with my instincts. It was sort of a fling on the wing. I had never done that before but now I have - but he is very unselfish in bed.

From Yves I have heard nothing - but I don't mind since I have such a strong, tender, wonderful memory.

I am almost weeping.....

Marilyn with Edith Sitwell, London, 1956
Marilyn with Carl Sandburg, Los Angeles, 1961

WRITTEN ANSWERS
TO AN INTERVIEW
1962

Whereas Marilyn often established bonds of trust and complicity with photographers, she was much more on her guard with journalists. That was why she prepared for interviews and often insisted on seeing the questions beforehand. That was obviously the case here, where we can read short draft answers she wrote to about thirty questions (the first few are missing) to give herself a lead. She invoked the master-pupil aspect of her relationship with Arthur Miller, and her difficulty in being a member of a group. No wonder that among the people she admired we find Eleanor Roosevelt (who was to die soon after Marilyn in November 1962), who was famous for her early feminism and opposition to racism, and who headed the U.N. commission to draw up the Universal Declaration of Human Rights. No less surprising was Marilyn's support for the Kennedy brothers, for their strength and youth and idealism. She also looked up to Carl Sandburg for his poetry, so sympathetic to the common man, as well as Greta Garbo, the other myth. A horrified vision of the H-bomb, support for all manner of persecuted people, a considered defense of psychoanalysis: the glamorous blonde was certainly no reactionary.

From her reference to Payne Whitney (where she had been confined for five days in February 1961) and from the books that the photographer George Barris, one of the last to shoot her, states she was reading a few days before her death, we may judge that these notes were written in 1962.

6-

Although this may be true
in my estimation of an ~formal~ educational
is _never_ a basic cause for a
material problem. it is the emotional
back~ground~ which matters

⑦ there was a pupil teacher, relationship
at the beginning of the ~marriage~ and
3 but there was much more to the ~marriage~ ~than that~ ~I~ learned a great deal from it.
⟹ A good marriage is a very delegate
balance of many forces.

⑩ experiences with any group of people is disalowing
one has to discriminate the different members of
a group. I never been very good at being
a member of any group — more than a group
of two that is. payne whitney gives me a pain
⑪ It was ~obody~ ~and~ error of judgment
to place me in payne Whit. And the doctor
who recomened ~it~ realyid it and tried
to rectify it. what the my condition
warranted was the rest and care I got
prospectern Hospital

6 – although this may be true in my estimation of a formal educational is <u>never</u> a basic cause for a material problem—it is the emotional back**ground** which matters

7 – (1) there was a pupil teacher relationship at the beginning of the marriage and ~~when~~ (2) I learned a great deal from it—a good marriage is a very **delicate** balance of many forces (3) but there was much more to the marriage than that

10 – experiences with any group of people is [illegible]
one has to discriminate the different members of a group. I never been very good at being a member of any group—more than a group of two that is.

11 – Payne Whitney gives me a pain
It was ~~often~~ obviously an error of judgment to place me in Payne Whit. and the doctor who recommended ~~it~~ realized it and tried to rectify it. What ~~the~~ my condition warranted was the rest and care I got **at** Presbyterian Hospital

12 the work and a few reliable human beings the love that a few reliable human beings the hope for my future growth & development.

13 I have a strong sense of self & criticism but I believe I'm becoming more reasonable and tolerant realistic in this regard

14 — Eleanor Roosevelt — her devotion to mankind
Carl Sandburg — His poems are songs of
Pres and the people by the people
and for people
Robert Kennedy — they symbolizes the youth
of America — in its vigor
its brilliance and its compassion
Greta Garbo — for her Artistic creativity and
her personal courage and integrity

15 I am at ease with people I trust or admire or like the rest I'm not at ease with.

16 — At the present time I'm reading
Capt Newman M.D. and To Kill a
mocking bird — in times of crisis
I do not turn to a book — I try to
think and to use my understanding

17 — I love poetry and poets

18 I constantly try to clarify and redefine
my goals

12 – the love of my work ~~I love~~ and a few reliable human beings
the hope for my future growth & development.

13 – I have a strong sense of self of criticism but I believe I'm <u>becoming</u> more
reasonable and tolerant **realistic** in this regard

14 – Eleanor Roosevelt—her devotion to mankind
Carl Sandburg—his poems are songs of the people by the people and for people
Pres. and Robert Kennedy—they symbolize the youth of America—in its vigor its
brilliance and its compassion
Greta Garbo—for her artistic creativity and her personal courage and integrity

15 – I am at ease with people I trust or admire or like the rest I'm not at ease with.

16 – At the present time I'm reading Capt. Newman M.D. and To Kill a Mockingbird—
in times of crisis I do not turn to a book—I try to think and to use my understanding

17 – I love poetry and poets

18 – I constantly try to clarify and redefine my goals

Notes:
Captain Newman, M.D. is a novel by Leo Rosten (no relation to Norman), published in 1961, based on the experiences of Ralph Greenson when he was a military officer at Yuma (Arizona) during the Second World War.
To Kill a Mockingbird, the Pulitzer Prize–winning novel by Harper Lee, was published in 1960.

In *Marilyn: Her Life in Her Own Words*, the photographer George Barris describes the conversation he had with her on August 3, 1962, the day before her death, when she told him she was reading these two books.

19   my sleep depends on my state of
satisfaction and that varies with my
life — my dreams are too intimate
to be revealed in public.
my nightmare is the H Bomb. whats
yours?
                                    answering personal   religious
20 (2) I have always ~~that~~ refrain from ~~teaching~~   ~~questions~~
   (1) I have great feeling for all the persecuted
   ones in the world.

21. I hope at some future time to be
able to make a glowing report about
the wonders that psychoanalysis can
achieve. the time is not ripe.

22 early a lack of sufficient training and experience
~~to offset til now~~

23. I would not wish to slight all the actresses
who would be left off such a list and
therefore refrain from answering

24. the lack of any consistant love and caring.
a mistrust and fear of the world was the result.
there were no benefits except what it could teach
me about the basic needs of the young, ~~the sick~~
and the weak.

25 I can't answer at this time
26 ~~yes~~ and I would underline it,
27 — in spades!

19 – my sleep depends on my state of satisfaction and that varies with my life—my dreams are too intimate to be revealed in public.
My nightmare is the H Bomb. What's yours?

20 – (1) I have great feeling for all the persecuted ones in the world
(2) But I ~~must~~ have always refrained from ~~discussing~~ answering personal religious questions.

21 – I hope at some future time to be able to make a glowing report about the wonders that psychoanalysis can achieve. The time is not ripe.

22 – Early lack of sufficient training and experience ~~as of yet until now~~

23 – I would not wish to slight all the actresses who would be left off such a list and therefore refrain from answering

24 – The lack of any consistent love and caring. A mistrust and fear of the world was the result. There were no benefits except what it could teach me about the basic needs of the young, the sick, and the weak.

25 – I can't answer at this time

26 – yes and I would underline it

27 – in spades!